This book belongs to:

Anxan

It was given to me by:

HEAVENLY

On:

01/13/24

3-Minute
BEDTIME PRAYERS
for Girls

Janice Thompson

BARBOUR **kidz**
A Division of Barbour Publishing

Published by Barbour Publishing, Inc., 1810 Barbour Drive, Uhrichsville, Ohio 44683, www.barbourbooks.com

Our mission is to inspire the world with the life-changing message of the Bible.

Member of the
Evangelical Christian
Publishers Association

Printed in China.

001695   0823   HA

May these words of mine, which I have prayed to the Lord, be near to the Lord our God day and night.

1 Kings 8:59

INTRODUCTION

The sun has already slipped over the horizon. The night-time sky is twinkling with shimmering stars as you climb into bed after a long day. When you put your head on the pillow, you doze off, ready to wake up fresh in the morning to begin again.

But before you drift off, don't forget to spend some time with Jesus. Thank Him for helping you through another day. Praise Him for all He's doing in your life. And let Him know that you trust Him—even with the big stuff you don't understand.

In this prayer book, you'll find 180 nighttime prayers that will help you draw closer to your heavenly Father—the one who created you and knows you best.

- First, take a minute to read the scripture verse.

- Then pray the prayer—from your heart.

- Finally, take a moment to think about what you've just read. God wants you to learn from this little book!

Your heavenly Father loves you most. You can trust Him, girl, even while you sleep!

YOU MADE IT ALL

In the beginning God made from nothing
the heavens and the earth.

GENESIS 1:1

You're amazing, God! You must have the best imagination ever! You made everything out of absolutely nothing. (How did You do that?) The world was like a blank piece of paper with nothing written on it, and You looked at it and wrote a whole story. And You made me part of that story. Thank You so much for being an amazing Creator! You were creating then, and You are creating now. You are always making everything new, and I'm so glad. Tonight, as I snuggle into bed, I want to thank You for all You've created. Amen.

—————— Think about it: ——————

If your teacher asked you to complete a science project, you couldn't start with nothing, could you? God started from nothing and made everything! He's the only one who could do that.

Let There Be Light

Then God said, "Let there be light," and there was light.
GENESIS 1:3

Lord, how did You do it? How did You look into the darkness, speak a few words, and cause everything to change? You said, "Let there be light" and—*poof!*—light appeared. Bright, shining light that drove the darkness away! That's amazing, Jesus! Your words changed everything during creation, and they're changing things now too. Thank You for speaking good words over my life! You're creating great things in me, and I'm so happy! Amen.

--------- Think about it: ---------

If God's words were powerful enough to create the sun, moon, and stars, isn't He powerful and trustworthy enough to take care of you, even while you're asleep?

THE DIVIDING LINE

God saw that the light was good.
He divided the light from the darkness.
GENESIS 1:4

God, as soon as You created the light, You looked at it and said, "That's good!" And it's *still* good. There's a lot of dark (bad) stuff in this world, and You're always telling me, "Stay away from that dark stuff, girl." So, I'll do it. I'll stay on the light side of things. I won't mess with lying, cheating, and hurting others. I want to live in the light every single day because I know it makes Your heart happy! Even if I messed up today, You can—and will!—help me do better tomorrow. Thanks for showing me how to live a light-bright life, Lord! Amen.

--------- Think about it: ---------

God took the time to divide the light from the dark. That means there's an obvious separation between the two. How can you be sure to stay on the right (light) side?

GOD'S NiGHt LiGHt

Then God made the two great lights, the brighter light to rule the day, and the smaller light to rule the night. He made the stars also.
GENESIS 1:16

I'll admit it, Father. Sometimes I still sleep with a night-light. It helps me if I get up in the middle of the night to get a drink of water. I won't trip and fall! It's not as bright as the big light in my room, but it's enough to help me see through the darkness. That night-light reminds me of the moon You hung in the night sky. You literally thought of *everything*, God. While I sleep, the moon and stars are shining brightly over me, gently lighting up the night sky. Thank You. Amen.

——————— Think about it: ———————

If the night sky had no moon or stars, what would happen? We need God's "night-light" to see our way through the dark.

THiS BeautifuL PLaNet

And God wanted good to come to them, saying, "Give birth to many. Grow in number. Fill the earth and rule over it. Rule over the fish of the sea, over the birds of the sky, and over every living thing that moves on the earth."
GENESIS 1:28

You love us so much, God! You created human beings to oversee the earth—to rule over the fish of the sea and the birds of the sky. You made us caretakers over the plants and the rivers, the mountains and the valleys. You put a lot of trust in us. Tonight, as I tuck myself in bed, I want to thank You for this beautiful planet that You gave us. I'll do my best to take care of it! Amen.

––––––––––––––– Think about it: –––––––––––––––

God could have put the rabbits or the giraffes in charge of the planet, but He chose humankind.
Why do you suppose He did that?

YOU MADE IT ALL, LORD

*Christ made everything in the heavens and on the
earth. He made everything that is seen and things
that are not seen. He made all the powers of heaven.
Everything was made by Him and for Him.*
COLOSSIANS 1:16

Father God, it's amazing that You made absolutely
everything. Fluffy clouds, slithering snakes, green grass,
mountain peaks, rushing rivers, yappy puppies—all of
them were Your idea! You have a great imagination.
When I get to heaven, I want to ask You some questions
about slithering snakes, biting ants, and pesky mosqui-
toes. But for now, I just want to thank You for making
all of creation. I trust You to take care of it all (and to
take care of me) as I sleep. Amen.

——————— Think about it: ———————

If God made everything, He can take care of
everything! Is God still hard at work taking care
of His creation, even while you're sleeping?

SHINING-GREATNESS!

"Our Lord and our God, it is right for You to have the shining-greatness and the honor and the power. You made all things. They were made and have life because You wanted it that way."
REVELATION 4:11

You deserve my praise, Jesus. There are lots of great people in my life, and I love them all, but You're the greatest of the greatest! You're the only one who created everything around me. No one else has that kind of power! You have the shining-greatness. You have the honor and power. You made everything! And You decided to make me (and everyone else I love) too! Tonight, I just want to thank You for who You are and all You've done. Amen.

—————— Think about it: ——————

There are lots of great people in your world but only one Creator! Does anyone else have the power that God has?

AN UNUSUAL WAY TO CREATE

Then the Lord God made man from the dust of the ground. And He breathed into his nose the breath of life. Man became a living being.
GENESIS 2:7

God, You chose a strange way to create men and women! You picked up some dust and breathed into it—and out of the dust came a man. Then You took a rib from the man while he was sleeping and turned it into a woman. You're a creative God! If You could do all that (turn something weird like dust into a human), then I know I can count on You to turn the not-so-great situations in my life around. Tonight, while I'm sleeping, I'll trust You with my problems. Amen.

——————— Think about it: ———————

God makes good things out of bad. And He never changes—so He's still turning bad into good! Do you trust Him to fix the tough stuff in your life?

A CLEAN HEART

*Make a clean heart in me, O God. Give me
a new spirit that will not be moved.*
PSALM 51:10

Some days my heart isn't very happy, Jesus. I get mad.
I get frustrated. I get worked up. I get jealous. I want
to say the wrong things and do the wrong things. Then
nighttime comes, and I feel sorry for how icky my heart
felt all day. I want to start over fresh tomorrow. I want
things to be different. So, tonight, before I go to sleep,
I give You the parts of my heart that weren't very pretty
today. If You created the sun, moon, and stars, I know
You can create a clean heart in me. Amen.

Think about it:

Every single moment of every single day God
is in the "creating" business. Will He give
you a new heart anytime you ask for it?

I WANT TO BE MORE LIKE YOU, JESUS

And God made man in His own likeness. In the likeness of God He made him. He made both male and female.
GENESIS 1:27

What do You look like, God? The Bible says You created humans in Your likeness. So, when I look in the mirror, am I seeing reflections of You? Do I have Your smile or Your kind heart? Do I have hopes and dreams that came from You? I want to be more like You, Lord. Tonight, as I rest my head on my pillow, please show me how I can be more like You, my heavenly Father. Tomorrow, may I show others just how wonderful You are by being a lovely reflection of You. Amen.

Think about it:

You're created in God's image, girl! So, can you think the way He thinks, love the way He loves, and speak the way He speaks?

YOU ARE SPIRIT

"God is Spirit. Those who worship Him must worship Him in spirit and in truth."
JOHN 4:24

Sometimes I wonder what You look like, God. I wonder if You have eyes and hair and hands and feet. Then I remember that the Bible says You are Spirit. Until I get to heaven, I won't ever see You face-to-face, but I can sense Your presence near me even when I'm sleeping. I don't have to see You to trust You. I don't have to touch You to know You're right here with me, even now, as I climb into bed and settle down for a good night's sleep. I trust You, my heavenly Father! Amen.

———————— Think about it: ————————

Do you have to "see" the wind to know it's blowing? Do you have to "see" the water in the pipes to know it will come out when you turn on the faucet?

YOU ARE LOVE

*Those who do not love do not know
God because God is love.*
1 JOHN 4:8

Some people I know aren't very loving, Father. (You know who I'm talking about.) The Bible says that You are love. And when we follow You, we learn to love others. I wonder if these not-so-nice people even know who You are. I guess I should be more patient with the people who aren't very loving. I will pray that they come to know You so they can learn how to love. And when I wake up in the morning, please show me how I can love people better too. Amen.

————— Think about it: —————

God is love. What good things happen
when you put your trust in Him?

YOU ARE THE ONLY WAY

Jesus said, "I am the Way and the Truth and the Life. No one can go to the Father except by Me."
JOHN 14:6

Some days, I just don't know which way to go. I make wrong decisions and end up feeling sorry for them. But You always help me correct my course so I can go in the right direction again. You're great with directions, Jesus! You lead and guide me all the way. I love this promise from Your Word. It says that You are the Way, the Truth, and the Life. (No wonder You're so great at guiding me!) You show me the way every single time. I'm so grateful! Amen.

————————— Think about it: —————————

Jesus is the only way to get to heaven. If He knows how to get you to heaven, doesn't He surely know how to guide you in your life?

YOU ARE THE FIRST AND LAST

"I am the First and the Last. I am the beginning and the end."
REVELATION 22:13

Jesus, You are the First and the Last, the beginning and the end. My day starts and ends with You. And You are here for every single moment in between. You're with me when I'm in school, struggling to fit in. You're with me when I'm arguing with my mom or with a sibling. You're right here when I'm trying to figure out how to do my homework. I'm so happy You're always with me, Jesus. Amen.

―――――――――― Think about it: ――――――――――

If Jesus created everything and is the beginning and end of everything, doesn't it make sense that He's always with you when you need Him?

YOU SENT YOUR SON TO SAVE US

We have seen and are able to say that the Father sent His Son to save the world from the punishment of sin.
1 JOHN 4:14

Jesus, I know why You came to the earth as a baby in a manger. I understand it now! You came to save us. You gave Your life for me so I could spend forever in heaven with You. I don't know how I can ever thank You for dying on the cross for me. Maybe the best thing I can do is live my life fully for You, loving others the way You have loved me. Tomorrow is a fresh start to do just that. Tonight, give me sweet rest so that I can wake up in the morning ready to love others. Thank You. Amen.

———— Think about it: ————

Jesus came to save you out of His great love for you. Why would He want you to show that love to others, even those who are hard to love?

YOU HAVE GIVEN US YOUR SPIRIT

*He has given us His Spirit. This is how we
live by His help and He lives in us.*
1 JOHN 4:13

Jesus, I keep thinking about how sad it must have been
for Your disciples after You went away to heaven. Were
they lonely? Did they lose their faith? It would be so sad
to lose a friend. But then I remember that You sent Your
Holy Spirit to live inside of them—and us. Your Spirit is a
comforter, a counselor, and a friend! I'm so glad I have
the Holy Spirit living inside of me to help me every day
of my life! Amen.

———————— Think about it: ————————

The Spirit of God is living inside of you right now!
If you need comforting, He's your comforter.
If you need wisdom, He can give you wisdom.
What do you need? Ask the Spirit of God to help you.

YOU DO IMPOSSIBLE THINGS

Jesus said, "God can do things men cannot do."
LUKE 18:27

Jesus, I could give You a whole list of things that I don't know how to do. Some things feel impossible to me. I try and try and just can't figure everything out. But You can do everything! You do impossible things. You tell storms to stop, and they do. You tell hearts to beat, and they do. You heal the sick, fix broken relationships, and even calm people down when they get mad. (I know, because You've done this for me when I couldn't do it myself.) There's *nothing* You can't do. So I'm going to trust You to do everything I can't. Amen.

——————— Think about it: ———————

If God could create the whole universe,
isn't He able to work other miracles too?

YOU NEVER CHANGE

*Jesus Christ is the same yesterday
and today and forever.*
HEBREWS 13:8

Today, I woke up in my pajamas. Then I changed into my clothes. Then I changed back into some pajamas. Some days, I change into a sports uniform or bathing suit. I change, change, change. And my attitude changes too. Some days, I'm happy; other days, I'm sad. Some days, I'm a hard worker; other days, I'm lazy. Some days, I say nice things to my family; other days, I'm rude to them. (I change all the time!) I'm so glad You're an unchanging God! I'm thankful that You're always the same loving heavenly Father no matter what. Amen.

—————— Think about it: ——————

God loved you even before you were born.
If He's the same yesterday, today, and forever,
don't you think He'll go on loving you forever?

Let Everything Praise You, Jesus!

*Let everything that has breath praise
the Lord. Praise the Lord!*
PSALM 150:6

Jesus, Your Word says that everything that has breath should praise You. I have breath. The animals have breath. Reptiles have breath. All sorts of living creatures breathe. Does this mean that they all praise You? If so, that's very cool! Tonight, before I go to sleep, I want to spend a couple of minutes praising You for all You've done for me. You've given me a family, a home, and food to eat. You're so good to me, and I want to say, "Thank You!" and "Praise You!" Amen.

———————— Think about it: ————————

Jesus said that if we don't praise God, the
rocks and stones will cry out (Luke 19:40).
Does everything on the planet praise Him?

THE WORDS I SPEAK

My mouth is filled with Your praise and with Your honor all day long.
PSALM 71:8

If I'm being honest, Jesus, I must admit that I don't spend every day praising You all day long. But I want to! When I see the sun come up in the morning, I will praise You. When my baby brother giggles and laughs, I'll praise You for that too! When I make a new friend, when I get a good grade, when Dad gets a raise at work—I'll praise You for all those things. No matter what I'm going through, You are worthy of my praise all day long! Amen.

——————— Think about it: ———————

Who causes good things to happen—you or God?

I Will Never Forget, Lord

*Praise the Lord, O my soul. And forget
none of His acts of kindness.*
PSALM 103:2

Okay, I'll admit it, Jesus. Sometimes I forget all the
good things You've already done for me: that time You
healed me when I was sick; that time You answered my
prayer about a school problem; that time I was angry
and upset. You made it all right again, and I forgot to
say thank You. I'm sorry for forgetting. Today, I'm going
to stop and praise You for the many, many times You've
come through for me! Amen.

——————— Think about it: ———————

God has fixed a lot of messes in your life already.
He's the great fixer! When was the last time
you praised Him for what He's already done?

I Will Sing Praises to You

"So I will give thanks to You among the nations, O Lord. I will sing praises to Your name."
2 Samuel 22:50

Sometimes I just feel like singing, Jesus. You put a song in my heart and I tra-la-la-la-la all day long. Other days, not so much. Thank You for putting a song of praise in my heart. Even on the bad days, You can turn things around by giving me a song of joy. When people see that I'm doing okay on the tough days, they will wonder why. And then I can tell them, "It's because of Jesus! He gives me joy even when times are hard." Thank You, Lord! Amen.

Think about it:

God understands the pain you go through. And He can give you a song of praise. How many lives do you think you can influence by responding with joy, even in hard situations?

I PRAISE YOU IN GOOD TIMES AND BAD

Is anyone among you suffering? He should pray.
Is anyone happy? He should sing songs of thanks to God.
JAMES 5:13

I have hard days sometimes, Jesus! They don't start out that way. I wake up happy and excited. Then something bad happens, and I get in a bad mood. Then things get worse, and my mood gets worse too. (Sorry!) Some days, things feel completely unfair! But then I read a verse like this one, and You remind me that even on the bad days, I can still have a good attitude. Even on the icky days, I can still sing a song of praise to You. No matter what tomorrow looks like—good or bad—I'm going to do my best to have a happy heart. Amen.

——————— Think about it: ———————

Who controls your heart?

YOU ARE WORTHY

Praise the Lord! Praise God in His holy place! Praise Him in the heavens of His power! Praise Him for His great works! Praise Him for all His greatness!
PSALM 150:1–2

I'm going to praise You everywhere, Jesus! At home, in my bedroom, in class, in the middle of a test, on the school bus, at the park, at church, even when I'm walking the dog. No matter where I am, You're there! No matter what I'm going through, You're still worthy of my praise. So I praise You tonight—before I drift off to sleep—for this life You've given me and for all the hundreds and thousands of ways You have blessed me. I praise You, Lord! Amen.

————————— Think about it: —————————

God is everywhere, so doesn't it make sense that you should praise Him everywhere?

I PRAISE YOU WITH INSTRUMENTS

Praise Him with the sound of a horn.
Praise Him with harps.
PSALM 150:3

Music is so fun, Jesus! I love singing. And I know You love it too! You also love instruments—horns, harps, and lots of other musical instruments besides! It's so fun to praise You with singing and playing a tune. Even when I don't feel like it, You can take my bad attitude and turn it around with a worship song I hear on the radio or a melody my mom is humming while she's doing the dishes. That's the power of praise! It changes everything. Thank You, Lord! Amen.

――――――― Think about it: ―――――――

God loves music, and He put that love inside of you too. What is your favorite way to use music to praise Him?

A Dance of Praise

Praise Him with timbrels and dancing.
Praise Him with strings and horns.
PSALM 150:4

Sometimes I just feel like dancing, Jesus. My toes start tapping, my hands start clapping, and before I know it, I'm dancing around the room. I get so excited that I want to celebrate by move-move-moving! I know You love it when we dance. This is one more way to praise You, and I love it too! So, next time I'm down in the dumps, I'm going to change my attitude. Instead of whining and moping, I'll just start dancing! Amen.

―――――― Think about it: ――――――

What happens when you're dancing? Are you worrying about the hard stuff or relaxing and having fun? Let go of your troubles and join the dance, girl!

THANK YOU, JESUS!

I will praise the name of God with song. And I will give Him great honor with much thanks.
PSALM 69:30

Sometimes I forget to say thanks. My mom cooks dinner and does the dishes, and I don't thank her. Clean clothes magically appear in my dresser drawers, and I take it for granted. My dad works hard, and I don't remember to say, "Thanks for all you do, Dad." My teachers work hard too, and I forget to say thanks. Sometimes I even forget to thank *You*, Jesus. Tomorrow, when I wake up, help me to remember all the many people I need to thank for all they've done for me! Amen.

——————— Think about it: ———————

It's so fun to have a grateful heart! Is it really possible to lift someone's spirits just by offering a smile and a quick "Thanks"?

PRaise isN't Always easy

Let us give thanks all the time to God through
Jesus Christ. Our gift to Him is to give thanks.
Our lips should always give thanks to His name.
HEBREWS 13:15

It's not always easy to praise You, Jesus. Some days (just keeping it real), I don't feel like it. I want to pitch a fit. I want to have my way. I want to prove a point. I want to get away from the people who are driving me crazy. I don't want to lift my hands in praise or sing or dance. But then I remember that these little fits of mine aren't healthy for me. I turn my attention away from myself and place it on You. And when I do that, I remember that You're amazing! You're the best! You're worthy of all my praise. I praise You, and everything changes! Amen.

————— Think about it: —————

It's kind of selfish to focus on "me, me, me"
all the time, isn't it? Turn your focus to "Jesus,
Jesus, Jesus" and see how things change.

YOUR KINGDOM COME

"May Your holy nation come. What You want done,
may it be done on earth as it is in heaven."

MATTHEW 6:10

I don't always want what You want, Jesus. I can't believe
I'm admitting that, but it's true. Sometimes I want things
for myself—new toys, new friends, new experiences—but
they're not what You want for me. Sometimes You don't
give me the things I want to protect me. (Sometimes
those new friends can lead me down a wrong path!)
Show me how to want what You want—for myself and
for others. Your kingdom come, Your will be done—in
my life and in the lives of those I love. Amen.

——————— Think about it: ———————

When is it good not to demand your own way
and let God control the situation instead?

I SEEK YOU FIRST

"First of all, look for the holy nation of God. Be right with Him. All these other things will be given to you also."
MATTHEW 6:33

Okay, I have something to confess, Jesus: I don't always put You first. Sometimes I put myself first. I want what I want, and I want it right now. I get a little selfish. Then I remember that if I put You first, You'll make sure I have everything I need (not everything I want, but everything I truly need). Tomorrow is a fresh new day, filled with possibilities. I want to wake up remembering that Your way is the best way. To be right with You means that everything else in my life will turn out all right. Help me rest tonight so that I can wake up refreshed and ready to put You first. Amen.

———————— Think about it: ————————

Whose way is the best way—yours or God's?

I Will Tell Everyone!

He kept on preaching about the holy nation of God. He taught about the Lord Jesus Christ without fear. No one stopped him.
ACTS 28:31

Sometimes I'm scared to talk to my friends about You, Jesus. Some of them don't believe in You, and they think I'm weird. Others say they believe, but they sure don't act like it. I'm sorry for the times I let them stop me from sharing the good news. Knowing You is the best thing ever, and I want everyone to know You too! So help me to be brave. Give me the right words for the right person so I can let them know how great You are. I want to be a good witness, Jesus—the very best! Give me courage. Amen.

——————— Think about it: ———————

If you had a miracle cure for cancer, you would tell everyone, right? The good news of what Jesus did on the cross is the best news ever! It's better than the best medicine!

Following After You

Then [Jesus] said to the crowd, "If any of you wants to be my follower, you must give up your own way, take up your cross daily, and follow me. If you try to hang on to your life, you will lose it. But if you give up your life for my sake, you will save it."
Luke 9:23–24 NLT

I don't always follow the right people, Jesus. Sometimes I just want to fit in, so I say what others say. I dress how they dress. I act like they act. I know You want me to be more like You and less like them, but I'm going to need Your help with this one for sure! To be a Jesus follower is the best thing in the world. So help me to stop being a people pleaser and to care more about what You think than what others think. Amen.

--- Think about it: ---

If you follow people, where will they lead you?
If you follow Jesus, where will He lead you?

GReat PLaNS!

" 'For I know the plans I have for you,' says the Lord, 'plans for well-being and not for trouble, to give you a future and a hope.' "
JEREMIAH 29:11

Sometimes I wish I could see into the future, Jesus! I don't know where I'm going or how I'm supposed to get there. I must trust that You know all that! You see the things I can't see. You've made plans for my life that I don't understand yet. It's kind of fun—like an adventure—to keep walking even when I don't know where I'm going. But I fully trust You. I know You have good things ahead, and that's enough for me! Thank You. Amen.

——————— Think about it: ———————

Has God ever let you down? Hasn't He already proven that His plans for you are good, not bad?

DON'T ACT LIKE THEM

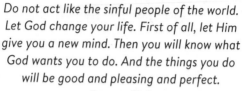

Do not act like the sinful people of the world.
Let God change your life. First of all, let Him
give you a new mind. Then you will know what
God wants you to do. And the things you do
will be good and pleasing and perfect.

ROMANS 12:2

Here I am again, Jesus, telling You something You already know. Sometimes I act like the kids I hang out with—and not when they're behaving in a good way. Sometimes I let them rub off on me. I don't mean to! I always say I'm going to be a good witness. But then something happens, and I want to fit in, so I go along with what they tell me to do. I always regret it. I always feel guilty afterward. Please help me start fresh tomorrow. Give me godly friends, and help us all to be more like You. Amen.

——————— Think about it: ———————

Jesus has surrounded you with amazing people who are doing the right things. Does it make sense to hang out with only the ones who are breaking His heart with their behaviors?

It All Works Out For Good

*We know that God makes all things work
together for the good of those who love Him
and are chosen to be a part of His plan.*
ROMANS 8:28

Jesus, some of the stuff that has happened to me doesn't feel good. Sometimes people hurt my feelings, or people I love go through hard situations. I've been through a lot of rough patches that really hurt. It's hard to imagine that You will work everything out for good. Even the broken friendships? Even the sickness and pain? Even the bad grades in school? Your Word promises You'll make everything right in the end, so I'm going to put my trust in You. No matter how rough the situation, I believe You'll turn it for good in my life. Amen.

—————— Think about it: ——————

When you look back over the tough things you've
been through, are those things still as bad as
they once were, or did God turn them around?
He's in the turning-things-around business!

GOD'S PLANS, NOT MINE

There are many plans in a man's heart,
but it is the Lord's plan that will stand.
PROVERBS 19:21

I have many things on my to-do list, Jesus! I'm a busy, busy girl. I love to do many different things and enjoy lots of activities. I'm also excited about the future. I have lots of plans for this year, next year, and even when I'm older. Sometimes I get so busy that I forget who's in charge of my plans! (I know You are!) Thank You for reminding me of that. I want to do the things You have planned for me. I know my life will be much easier if I put You in charge. Amen.

—————— Think about it: ——————

Who's in charge of your life? Who's the real decision-maker? Isn't it time to let God be the boss of you?

WHICH WAY DO I GO?

Your Word is a lamp to my feet and a light to my path.
PSALM 119:105

Sometimes I don't know what to do, Jesus. I don't know which way to go. Making decisions is hard! I don't want to mess up. Then I remember that You're lighting my path with Your Word (the Bible). When I'm confused, I can read the Bible, and it will help me make the right decisions. Even when I'm really confused, Your Word will guide me. Thank You for giving us the Bible so we know how to make good choices! Amen.

—————— Think about it: ——————

The Bible is like a lamp (or a light). What happens when you turn off a light? You stumble around in the dark, right? Isn't that what happens when you forget to read your Bible?

EVEN WHEN I DON't Get It

*Trust in the Lord with all your heart, and do
not trust in your own understanding.*
PROVERBS 3:5

I'm learning to trust You, Jesus, even when I don't understand what's going on. Things happen, and I can't figure
them out. I try so hard, but they make no sense to me
at all! Like that time my grandma got really sick. Or
that time my friend's parents got a divorce. Or that
time I got blamed for something I didn't do. Bad stuff
happens, and I want to figure it out and fix it right away!
But even when I can't understand it, and even when I
can't fix it, I can still trust You. I don't have to "get it"
to keep on trusting. Amen.

———————— Think about it: ————————

God's ways are higher than yours.
He knows things you don't. Can you fully
trust Him even when life makes no sense?

THE GOLDEN RULE

"Do to others as you would have them do to you."
LUKE 6:31 NIV

My idea of "do unto others" isn't always the same as Yours, Jesus! Sometimes I want to get even with people who hurt me. I want to embarrass or hurt them (just keeping it real!) because they hurt me first. But You want me to live differently. You want me to treat other people the way I *want* to be treated. Oh my. That changes everything! I want to be treated well. For sure, I want to be included. So I guess that means I must treat others kindly even when it's hard. Amen.

—————— Think about it: ——————

If you really treated people the way you wanted to be treated, what would change?

EVERYONE NEEDS JESUS

"I tell you, My Father in heaven does not want one of these little children to be lost."
MATTHEW 18:14

You're like a shepherd, Jesus, taking care of Your sheep. If one runs away, You leave the others to go find it. You care that much. You don't want anyone to be lost. You want everyone on the planet to fall in love with You and end up in heaven together. If You care that much about people, I should probably start caring more about them too. Show me how to reach others with the gospel message so that one day we can all experience the beauty of heaven together. Amen.

—————— Think about it: ——————

If God cares about the salvation of every single person on the planet, shouldn't you care too? Tonight, as you rest your head on your pillow, pray for those who don't know Him yet.

YOU OWN It All, Jesus!

And my God will give you everything you need because of His great riches in Christ Jesus.
PHILIPPIANS 4:19

You own everything, Jesus! You're like the richest person on the planet—but a gazillion times more! Everything I can see with my eyes belongs to You. Sometimes I know my parents worry about money. They wish they had more of it. But I know we can trust You to make sure we have everything we need because You own everything! Thank You for the promise from Your Word that You share Your riches with Your kids! Amen.

—————— Think about it: ——————

God is your good, good Father. Can you count on Him for everything?

WORRYWART!

"Do not worry. Do not keep saying, 'What will we eat?' or, 'What will we drink?' or, 'What will we wear?' The people who do not know God are looking for all these things. Your Father in heaven knows you need all these things."
MATTHEW 6:31–32

I'll admit it, Jesus! Sometimes I'm a worrywart. I worry about all sorts of silly things (and some serious things too). I worry about whether people will like me. I worry about school stuff. I worry about my siblings and my parents. Sometimes I even worry about all the stuff I wish I had. Then I remember that the Bible says, "Don't worry! Just trust God!" Whew! I can put my trust in You, Lord! Thanks so much. Amen.

——————— Think about it: ———————

How many minutes a day do you spend worrying about stuff? Does most of the bad stuff you worry about ever actually happen?

YOU KEEP YOUR PROMISES

"You are bad and you know how to give good things to your children. How much more will your Father in heaven give good things to those who ask Him?"
MATTHEW 7:11

I'm so glad You're not like the people I know, God! They say one thing, but then they do something else. They make promises and don't keep them. They let me down. You? You never let me down. If You say it, You'll do it! You're a wonderful Father who treats me with so much love! I'm grateful that You're looking out for me and that You do what You say You'll do. Amen.

——————— Think about it: ———————

Is God human? No way! Is He the Creator of everything (including you, girl)?

YOU GIVE US EVERYTHING WE NEED

*"Look at the birds. They do not plant seeds.
They do not gather grain. They have no grain
buildings for keeping grain. Yet God feeds them.
Are you not worth more than the birds?"*
LUKE 12:24

Whoa, what a cool verse, Jesus! You give the birds absolutely everything they need. They're up there singing in the trees, completely satisfied, because You give them food, water, and even other birds to hang out with. You're so good to Your creation! If I can trust You to take care of nature, You'll definitely take care of me! Amen.

——————— Think about it: ———————

The birds don't even have to ask God to meet their needs. He sees, and He acts! He provides everything they need. Doesn't God care about *you* even more?

WANTS AND NEEDS

The Lord is my Shepherd. I will have everything I need.
PSALM 23:1

I have a lot of stuff, but I'm always wanting more, more, more. My friends have lots of cool stuff, and sometimes I feel a little jealous. But then I remember that You've given me a good place to live, food on my plate, and clothes to wear. You've also given me people who love me, and that's good enough for me, God! Tonight, as I settle into bed, I'm feeling super grateful for all You've given me today. Thanks for taking such good care of me! Amen.

——————— Think about it: ———————

God promises to give you what you need,
not what you want. Do you have a hard time
figuring out which is which sometimes?

Mean Girls

"Respect and give thanks for those who try to bring bad to you. Pray for those who make it very hard for you."
LUKE 6:28

Can I be honest, Jesus? There are some girls at my school who aren't nice to me. They say rude things. They talk behind my back. Some of them pretend to be my friend to my face, but then, later, I find out they've said mean things behind my back. They gossip about me and tell stories that aren't true. I don't want to be kind to these mean girls, but the Bible says I should. It's hard, and I'm really going to need Your help. Show me how to react to the mean girls in a way that pleases You, Jesus. Amen.

─────── Think about it: ───────

Lots of people were mean to Jesus.
How did He treat them?

DON'T GO THERE

Do not have anything to do with a man given to anger, or go with a man who has a bad temper. Or you might learn his ways and get yourself into a trap.
PROVERBS 22:24–25

Sometimes I get confused, Jesus. I think the Bible is telling me I must be friends with everyone. But then I read verses like this one, and I see that You don't want me to be close friends with some people. I must love them and forgive them when they hurt me, but You don't want or expect me to link arms with them and become BFFs. Show me which people to draw close to and which ones to avoid so I don't make the mistake of being influenced by those with bad tempers and other negative qualities. Amen.

———————— Think about it: ————————

You can forgive the mean girls without getting too close to them. Which girls should you avoid?

Living in Peace with Others

*When the ways of a man are pleasing
to the Lord, He makes even those who
hate him to be at peace with him.*
PROVERBS 16:7

Some girls and boys are just hard to be around, Jesus. They are hotheaded and mean. They lie. They cheat. They pretend to be good in front of our teachers and other grown-ups, but they're really not who they pretend to be. I know You're watching and You see it, Lord. They're not easy to get along with. But Your Word promises that if I will have a peaceful attitude, they will simmer down. And so I choose to be a peacemaker, Lord. I want to make things better, not worse. Amen.

—————— Think about it: ——————

When someone starts acting angry and
you react with anger, what happens? What
happens if you choose peace instead?

EVERYTHING HAS ITS TIME

There is a time to cry, and a time to laugh;
a time to have sorrow, and a time to dance.
ECCLESIASTES 3:4

There's a time for everything, Jesus. I've learned this the hard way. There are days when I feel like crying all day long. Then, the very next day, I'm all smiles. There are days when I'm filled with energy and feel like I can do anything. Then the next day, I'm so tired I can barely get out of bed! I don't know what kind of day tomorrow is going to be, but as I climb into bed tonight, I want to thank You ahead of time. Whatever happens tomorrow, I know it will happen according to Your perfect plan. Amen.

─────── Think about it: ───────

Does God know what's going to happen tomorrow? Can you trust Him with that?

WHERE ARE MY RICHES?

"Your heart will be wherever your riches are."
LUKE 12:34

I'll admit it, Jesus. Sometimes my heart isn't in the right place. I get hung up on all the things I wish I had. Electronics. Toys. Clothes. Shoes. "Stuff" becomes too important to me. I chase after things too much. Thank You for reminding me that You are my treasure. I need to chase after You, not the things this world has to offer. I don't want to give my heart to the treasures of this world. Today I choose to give it only to You. Amen.

―――――― Think about it: ――――――

What do you spend your money on? Is it stuff that brings glory to God? Remember that wherever your treasure is, that's where your heart is too. Make sure it's focused on Jesus, not things.

ONLY YOU, GOD

"Have no gods other than Me."
EXODUS 20:3

Sometimes I read this verse and wonder what You mean, Lord. You're the only true God, after all! Then I remember that sometimes I make other things more important than You. Friendships. Grades. Talents. Possessions. I spend a lot of time thinking about those things instead of focusing on You. Thanks for reminding me that You are the most important thing in my life—You, and only You. I won't put anything ahead of You, Jesus! Tomorrow is a fresh, new day, and I will do my best with Your help. Amen.

—————— Think about it: ——————

Is there anything in your life that you put ahead of Jesus? Friendships? Sports? Possessions? Tonight, before you go to sleep, ask Him to forgive you, and start fresh tomorrow.

I WILL BE A JOY TO YOU

The Lord hates lying lips, but those
who speak the truth are His joy.
PROVERBS 12:22

I don't always tell the truth, Jesus. Sometimes I fib a little. I try to get away with things, by leaving out parts of the story. It's hard to be truthful all the time! Please forgive me for not always being honest. I want to be a joy to You. I know it makes You sad when I'm not completely truthful. Tomorrow is a brand-new day. Help me do my best so that I can bring You happiness by the way I live and the words I speak. Amen.

——————— Think about it: ———————

Would you consider yourself an honest person? Is there someone in your life who you have a hard time being honest with? Today you can ask Jesus to help you bring joy to His heart by speaking the truth even when it's hard.

GUARDING MY WORDS

A poor man who walks with honor is better
than a fool who is sinful in his speaking.
PROVERBS 19:1

My mouth gets me in trouble a lot, Jesus. (You already know this, of course!) Even today, I messed up and said some things I shouldn't have. My words weren't the kindest or the most helpful. I'm so glad You can forgive me for my not-so-great words. Tomorrow, I'm going to do my best to speak words that will please Your heart. I want to make You happy, and I want to bless the people I speak to as well. Please help me! Amen.

—————— Think about it: ——————

Your words have power. Do you use them for good
or for evil? Do they cause pleasure or pain?

A GiRl After God's Own Heart

The man said, "You must love the Lord your God
with all your heart. You must love Him with all your
soul. You must love Him with all your strength.
You must love Him with all your mind. You must
love your neighbor as you love yourself."
LUKE 10:27

I love, love, *love* my family. I love my friends. I love so many things in life, Jesus! But most of all, I love You. I don't always show it in the way I act (sorry about that!), but I really do. You are the most important part of my life. I wouldn't be here without You. Tonight, as I climb into bed, I want to go to sleep with these words on my lips: "I love You best, and I love You most, Lord!" Amen.

Think about it:

It's good to love your family and your friends.
It's great to love your pets and your neighbors.
God has shown you how to love all of them!
Who should you love above all others?

HOW TO TREAT YOUR ENEMIES

"If the one who hates you is hungry, feed him.
If he is thirsty, give him water. If you do that,
you will be making him more ashamed of himself."
ROMANS 12:20

I don't always feel like treating my enemies kindly, Jesus. But You tell me I need to go out of my way to be kind to the very people who are unkind to me. I'm definitely going to need Your help with this one. Some of the girls (and boys) I know are pretty mean to me. I don't feel like going out of my way to be kind to them. But I'll try it Your way. Help me have a good night's sleep so that I wake up tomorrow ready to love everyone—even the ones who are mean. Amen.

———————— Think about it: ————————

If you treated someone badly and they responded by blessing you anyway, how would that make you feel?

LOVE MY ENEMIES? REALLY?

"I say to you who hear Me, love those who work against you. Do good to those who hate you. Respect and give thanks for those who try to bring bad to you. Pray for those who make it very hard for you."
LUKE 6:27–28

It's not easy to love and respect those who are mean to me, Jesus, but You already know that. You went through it too. People were really mean to You, but You loved them anyway. In fact, You loved them so much that You gave Your life for them. That's true love! Help me as I face my enemies. Show me how to love them well. Show me how to give thanks for the ones who cause trouble for me. I can only do this with Your help. Amen.

——————— Think about it: ———————

If Jesus gave His life for his enemies, doesn't it make sense that He wants you to learn to love your enemies too?

YOU'RE BIGGER, GOD

*God is able to do much more than we ask or
think through His power working in us.*
EPHESIANS 3:20

You're bigger, God. You're bigger than my problems. You're bigger than that girl who has been bullying me. You're bigger than that math test I'm nervous about. Instead of fretting over how big my problems are, I'm going to start focusing on how much bigger You are. You are a miracle-working God who is able to do so much more than I can even imagine. Thank You! Amen.

─────── Think about it: ───────

If God created the heavens and the earth,
can't He surely take care of the problems
you're facing—even the super-huge ones?

I Will Mimic My Father

*Do as God would do. Much-loved children
want to do as their fathers do.*
EPHESIANS 5:1

Playing follow-the-leader is a lot of fun. But sometimes I accidentally play it in real life. I follow people who aren't great leaders. I let them lead me down the wrong path. Then I remember that the only leader I should follow is You, Jesus. You know where You're going, so I can trust You on the journey. I will do as You do. I will go where You go. I won't follow anyone else but You alone, Lord. Amen.

——————— Think about it: ———————

Who do you most want to be like? A
particular friend? A sibling? A parent? Isn't
chasing after Jesus your best bet, girl?

A PROMISE FROM YOU, GOD

Respect your father and mother. This is the first Law given that had a promise. The promise is this: If you respect your father and mother, you will live a long time and your life will be full of many good things.
EPHESIANS 6:2–3

This is an interesting promise, Jesus! If I respect my parents, I can have a long life filled with good things. It makes sense, though. The things Mom and Dad tell me to do are for my own good and for my safety. When they say, "Don't hang with the wrong kind of friends," it's because they know bad friends can lead to destruction. So I'll stick with Mom and Dad—and stick with You, Lord. I'll respect my parents and the other adults in my life, and I'll learn to walk in Your ways. Amen.

——————— Think about it: ———————

If you didn't respect your parents, what would happen? Would you end up going down a good path or a bad one?

WHO AM I FiGHTiNG?

Our fight is not with people. It is against the leaders and
the powers and the spirits of darkness in this world.
It is against the demon world that works in the heavens.
EPHESIANS 6:12

Sometimes I forget that people aren't my enemy, Jesus. But the devil certainly is! He causes people to say and do ugly things, and I lash out at them, forgetting that he's the one I should be mad at. Tomorrow, as soon as I wake up, remind me that any battles I face will be against him, not against other people. I won't take out my frustration or anger on my sister, my teacher, or my friends. I'll just let the devil know, once and for all, that he needs to stop messing with this girl! I'm a daughter of the King, after all! Amen.

--------- Think about it: ---------

When someone says something awful to you, who put those words in their mouth? Do you think they came up with those mean words all on their own, or was the devil behind them?

CARING FOR OTHERS

Be willing to help and care for each other because
of Christ. By doing this, you honor Christ.
EPHESIANS 5:21

I love the people who care about and for others, Jesus!
Mothers are like that. And fathers too. Grandparents
have the caring gene, and so do my teachers. I have a lot
of friends and family members who care about me a lot
too. Tomorrow, when I dress for my day, remind me to
put on "caring" so I can care more about those around
me. I want to be others-focused, not me-focused. Help
me to care about others just as You do, Jesus. Amen.

─────────── Think about it: ───────────

If people all stopped caring about each other,
what kind of world would this be? Who would help
during hard times? When you care for others,
it's almost like you're caring for Jesus Himself.

WATCH YOUR MOUTH, GIRL!

Do not be guilty of telling bad stories and of foolish talk. These things are not for you to do. Instead, you are to give thanks for what God has done for you.

EPHESIANS 5:4

I try so hard to watch the words that come out of my mouth, Jesus. I really do. Then I get upset and spout off. Or I find myself in a group of friends who are gossiping. Or I slip up and say something negative when I should be more positive. In other words, my mouth gets me in trouble. I even messed up a few times today. Tomorrow, please take control of my speech! Guard it. Watch it closely. I don't want to use my mouth to hurt others. Instead, I want my words to bring life and joy to all who I meet. Amen.

—————— Think about it: ——————

If your mouth is a weapon, how do you use it—for good or for evil?

THE BEST USE OF MY TIME

Make the best use of your time. These are sinful days.
EPHESIANS 5:16

I'll admit it, Jesus—I don't always make the best use of my time. Some days I waste a lot of time. I don't do it on purpose, but it happens. I sit down to watch a show, and three hours later I'm still sitting there. I call my friend on the phone, and we're still talking an hour later. I don't always value time the way You do. When I wake up tomorrow morning, please help me keep a good schedule—one that pleases Your heart! I don't want to waste one minute! Amen.

———————— Think about it: ————————

Why do you suppose the author of Ephesians added the line "These are sinful days" when talking about making the best use of your time? Could it be that the enemy is trying to steal precious time from you?

Always Means Always!

Always give thanks for all things to God the Father in the name of our Lord Jesus Christ.
EPHESIANS 5:20

Always means always, Lord. Every single day, in every single circumstance, You expect me to give thanks. When I'm happy and when I'm sad, when I'm hurting and when I'm mad. When people have treated me unfairly and unkindly. When I'm making great grades or when I'm failing. No matter what's swirling around me, You want the words on my lips to be "I praise You!" So tonight, as I crawl into bed, I say it one last time before I close my eyes: the day is done, but my praise goes on all through the night! Amen.

─────── Think about it: ───────

What makes you feel better—whining and complaining or having a grateful heart?

patience is hard!

My Christian brothers, you should be happy when you have all kinds of tests. You know these prove your faith. It helps you not to give up. Learn well how to wait so you will be strong and complete and in need of nothing.

JAMES 1:2–4

I wasn't very patient today, Jesus. I'm sure You saw how I behaved. When I want something, I usually want it right away. If I don't get what I want—well, You know. I sometimes get cranky. Then I read a verse like this one from the book of James, and I'm reminded that You want me to be patient no matter how long it takes. I'm definitely going to need Your help with this. Even if the answers don't come tomorrow, give me the patience to hang on until they do. Amen.

Think about it:

How patient has God been with you? Has He waited for you to do the right thing? Maybe it's time to learn from His example.

Wait FOR It

*But if we hope for something we do not yet
see, we must learn how to wait for it.*

ROMANS 8:25

I know what happens when I plant a seed in the ground,
Jesus. It doesn't grow today or even tomorrow. It takes
days—sometimes weeks—for that tiny seed to grow and
blossom. After that seed disappears into the dirt, my
faith journey begins! I have to trust that while I'm waiting,
You're working below the surface. Although I can't see
what's happening under there, I trust You—even when
I'm waiting, waiting, waiting for something to happen.
You will take that seed and make it grow. All I must do
is wait and believe. Amen.

——————— Think about it: ———————

God is a master gardener. He knows how
to make seeds grow. Even though you
can't see what's happening under the
soil, don't you trust that He can?

I'M GROWING UP!

When I was a child, I spoke like a child. I thought like a child. I understood like a child. Now I am a man. I do not act like a child anymore.

1 Corinthians 13:11

I've changed a lot over the last few years, Jesus. My face has changed. My hair has changed. My body has changed. My clothing choices have changed. Even the things I like to eat have changed! I'm growing up! When I was a little girl, I did silly little-girl things, but now that I'm getting older, I'm doing my best not to be too childish. I want to be more like You. I've heard that people do most of their growing while they sleep, so watch over me tonight as I grow, grow, grow! Amen.

——————— Think about it: ———————

What if babies never grew up? What if they never changed? That would be weird, right? God is always changing you for the better.

EVERY DAY OF MY LIFE

Bring up a child by teaching him the way he should go, and when he is old he will not turn away from it.
PROVERBS 22:6

I've learned so much about You, Jesus. From the time I was little until now, I've been taught that You love me, You care about my problems, and You have a plan for my life. I've learned that You have a wonderful place called heaven where I will one day live with other believers. (I'm so excited! It sounds wonderful!) Most of all, I have learned that You want me to love You back. So I promise to stick with You and love You no matter how old I get. Thanks for teaching me about Your love, Lord. Amen.

———————— Think about it: ————————

Do you think it's an accident that you are reading this little book? God has big plans for you, girl! He wants to remind you that He's with you every day of your life!

GROWING IN YOUR LOVING-FAVOR

*Grow in the loving-favor that Christ gives you.
Learn to know our Lord Jesus Christ better. He is
the One Who saves. May He have all the shining-
greatness now and forever. Let it be so.*
2 PETER 3:18

I'm not just growing up, Jesus—I'm growing in Your loving-favor. The more I know You, the more time I spend with You, the more my love for You grows and the more I see how much You love me. I'm Your special child. You adore me. That makes me feel very special. Before I go to sleep tonight, I just want to say thank You for pouring out Your loving-favor on me. Amen.

─────── Think about it: ───────

How do you know Jesus loves you?
How do you really, truly know? Can you sense
His love for you even on hard days?

A HOPEFUL FUTURE

" 'For I know the plans I have for you,' says the Lord, 'plans for well-being and not for trouble, to give you a future and a hope.' "

JEREMIAH 29:11

I love to think about what I'll be like in a few years, Jesus. It's so crazy to think about what I'll look like. How tall will I be? How big will my feet get? Will I have the same friends—or will they be different? What sort of job will I have one day? I have so much fun imagining. Of course, You already know the answers to those questions. You see into my future (cool!), and You know everything. Your Word says I have a "hopeful" future, so that means You must have big things ahead for me. I can't wait! Amen.

Think about it:

Do you trust Jesus with your future? What are you most excited about? He'll be right there with you, every step of the way!

YOU FINISH WHAT YOU START

*I am sure that God Who began the good
work in you will keep on working in you until
the day Jesus Christ comes again.*

PHILIPPIANS 1:6

You always finish what You start, Jesus. You don't start a puzzle and decide not to add the last few pieces. You know right where they fit! That's how I know I can trust You to finish the good works You've started in me. You never fail. You *always* come through! And so I'll be patient and trust You. I know You're always at work. Amen.

—————— Think about it: ——————

Would God start something and then give up halfway through? Of course not! He created the whole universe, not half. He created a whole giraffe, not half. Do you trust that He won't stop halfway with you either?

MANY PLANS

*There are many plans in a man's heart,
but it is the Lord's plan that will stand.*
PROVERBS 19:21

It's exciting, Lord! I have so many plans! I want to travel. I want to visit friends. I want to go to amusement parks. I want to go on a family vacation to the Grand Canyon. When it comes to school and learning, I want to go far! I want to learn. I want to go to college. I want to get a great job doing what I love. Whew! Lots of plans in my future. But then I remember that it's Your plans that *really* matter, Jesus. Thanks for having good plans for my life! Amen.

─────── Think about it: ───────

Whose plans are more important—yours or God's?

Gentleness

They must not speak bad of anyone, and they must not argue. They should be gentle and kind to all people.

Titus 3:2

I'm not always gentle, Jesus. Sometimes I'm a little harsh! I blow up at people and then regret it. I make fast decisions that aren't always wise. I get a little bossy. I don't want to be like this. I know that Jesus followers are meant to be gentle and kind to everyone. (Why is that always hardest with the people I love the most?) Help me, please. I want to be more like You—gentle, sweet, and patient with others. Amen.

--------- Think about it: ---------

Is Jesus gentle with you? When was the last time He treated you gently when you probably deserved discipline?

A Gentle Answer

A gentle answer turns away anger,
but a sharp word causes anger.
PROVERBS 15:1

I have two choices when someone is mean to me, Jesus: I can either be mean in return, or I can turn the other cheek. You want me to turn the other cheek, to overlook the mean thing she did. It would be easier to say something horrible, honestly. But that's not Your way, is it? Your way is the harder but better way. And, in the end, it's the way that leads to life and peace. I'll do it Your way, Jesus. Amen.

——————— Think about it: ———————

If Jesus went around being angry at everyone all the time, would people think He was a very good person? A gentle person wins more people over. An angry person pushes them away.

set Apart

*Your heart should be holy and set apart for
the Lord God. Always be ready to tell everyone
who asks you why you believe as you do.
Be gentle as you speak and show respect.*
1 Peter 3:15

You want me to be different than other people, don't
You, Jesus? I'm not supposed to go along with the crowd.
I've been set apart to do great things for You. That's
why it's so important that I guard what I say and do. It's
why I can't overreact to every little thing—because I'm
representing You. When people ask me, "Why are you
always smiling?" I will say, "It's because of Jesus!" Thank
You for making me Your child. Amen.

——————— Think about it: ———————

God chose you! You're so special to Him. Why
is it important that you represent Him well?

RaNDOM ActS OF KiNDNESS

You must be kind to each other. Think of the other person. Forgive other people just as God forgave you because of Christ's death on the cross.

EPHESIANS 4:32

It's so much fun to surprise people by doing nice things for them, Jesus. I'm always trying to think up clever ways to bring a smile to the faces of those I love. Tomorrow is a fresh, new day filled with excitement and adventure. When I wake up in the morning, please show me who I can bless. Give me creative ideas. Maybe I can write a kind note to someone or a thank-you to my teacher. Maybe I could help Mom fold the laundry *before* she asks for my help. There are so many ways I can offer random acts of kindness. What fun! Amen.

——————— Think about it: ———————

God showed you the best act of kindness ever when He sent His Son. What are some creative ways you can show kindness to others?

BE KIND TO THE UNKIND

*"But love those who hate you. Do good to them.
Let them use your things and do not expect something
back. Your reward will be much. You will be the
children of the Most High. He is kind to those who
are not thankful and to those who are full of sin."*
LUKE 6:35

Okay, I'll admit it—it's a lot easier being kind to those who are kind to me. Even today, I struggled to treat some not-so-nice people kindly. But Your Word says I must give kindness away to everyone I meet—no matter how they treat me. Ouch. Tomorrow is a fresh, new day, and I know I'll probably run into people who treat me badly. Show me how to bless them with random acts of kindness, Lord, even if I don't feel like it! Amen.

——————— Think about it: ———————

If Jesus was only kind to you when you were
behaving well, how often would He be kind to
you? Aren't you glad He's kind all the time?

I Can Show Pity

The man who shows loving-kindness does himself good, but the man without pity hurts himself.
PROVERBS 11:17

It's difficult to watch the people I love go through hard stuff, Jesus. Sometimes it breaks my heart. I have a lot of pity for people who are hurting. I guess that's because my heart is like Your heart. I'm sure You have a lot of pity for Your kids who are hurting. The sick ones. The lonely ones. The heartbroken ones. The hungry ones. Those who don't have a home to live in or proper clothes and shoes to wear. If it breaks Your heart, it breaks my heart. Thank You for making me more like You. Amen.

--- Think about it: ---

Does your heart break for people who are hurting? If you're like Jesus, you should feel great compassion and pity for them.

FILLED WITH JOY

*Our hope comes from God. May He fill you with joy
and peace because of your trust in Him. May your
hope grow stronger by the power of the Holy Spirit.*
ROMANS 15:13

Sometimes I feel like a cup, Jesus. I'm filled up with joy
on most days, but some days I feel empty. I can't find
my joy anywhere. I'm so glad You're the giver of joy.
You give it and never take it away. When my cup feels
low, I come to You! Tomorrow morning when I wake up,
give me a full cup so there's plenty to spill over onto my
friends and family. May I be a joy-spreader everywhere
I go! Amen.

Think about it:

With Jesus in your life, is it really possible to
always have a cup overflowing with joy?

REPRESENT JESUS WITH JOY

*Be full of joy always because you belong to
the Lord. Again I say, be full of joy!*
PHILIPPIANS 4:4

Your Word says that I look like You, Jesus. I'm made in
Your image. My attitude needs to be like Your attitude.
I know that You are filled with joy, and that means I
should be too. I don't want people to see me looking
sour and depressed. Will they think You look like that?
No way! I'll keep on my happy face so they know You're
filled with joy too. Amen.

——————— Think about it: ———————

Do you look like Jesus in all you do and say, or are
you showing people a different picture of Him than
you should? It's time to look like Him—filled with joy!

Take Your Medicine!

A glad heart is good medicine, but a
broken spirit dries up the bones.
PROVERBS 17:22

How many times have I heard someone say, "Take your medicine"? If I forget to take my medicine when I'm sick, I won't get well. It's the same thing with joy. Joy is like medicine for my heart. It makes my heart glad. When I'm sad, it feels like I'm sick with the flu. But a little joy goes a long, long way in making me feel better. Tomorrow, when I wake up, fill my heart with joy so that I can share it with others who need cheering up. Amen.

——————— Think about it: ———————

Do you know someone who's sad? Maybe God would like you to share some joy with the one who's hurting. In what ways can you share the joy of Jesus?

MY JOY JAR

*"I have told you these things so My joy may
be in you and your joy may be full."*
JOHN 15:11

Sometimes my attitude sways back and forth, depending
on how I feel, Jesus. And sometimes how I feel changes
a lot depending on how people treat me. The words they
say can either hurt me or help me. I love the helpers,
the givers. When they say nice things, it's easier to be
joyful. Help me to keep my joy jar full even when not-
so-great words are spoken over me. Amen.

--------- Think about it: ---------

Does God want your emotions to go up and down?
Does He want you to be in the depths of despair
one minute and filled with joy the next? Or does
He want your joy jar to be full at all times?

POWER, LOVE, AND A GOOD MIND

*For God did not give us a spirit of fear. He gave us
a spirit of power and of love and of a good mind.*

2 TIMOTHY 1:7

You don't want me to be afraid, Jesus. Sometimes I forget that. There were a couple of times today when I forgot. But Your Word says that You didn't give me a spirit of fear, so I know those feelings weren't from You. When I get scared, I need to remember that You have given me a different spirit—one of power, love, and a good mind—so that I won't panic. I won't flip out and hide, quivering under the covers. I'll face those fears head-on in Jesus' name! Amen.

——————— Think about it: ———————

If fear doesn't come from God, then who—or where—
does it come from? You have a very real enemy,
girl, and he wants to trip you up. Don't let him!

YOU'RE NOT HARD TO FIND, JESUS

*I looked for the Lord, and He answered
me. And He took away all my fears.*
PSALM 34:4

Oh, there You are, Jesus! You've been right next to me
the whole time. How often I forget! I go looking for You,
thinking You're far away, but You're never more than a
heartbeat away from me. Best of all, when I cry out to
You, You answer! And when You do, my fears disappear—
poof! They're all gone, like a puff of wind blowing by.
Thank You for sticking so close and for taking care of
my scaredy-cat moments. You're the best, Jesus! Amen.

——————— Think about it: ———————

If God is always right next to you, then what do you
have to be afraid of? Nothing, right? When Jesus
lives in your heart, He's as close as your next breath!

I WON'T LOSE FAITH

"Have I not told you? Be strong and have strength of heart! Do not be afraid or lose faith. For the Lord your God is with you anywhere you go."

JOSHUA 1:9

Sometimes I get scared because I forget to have faith, Jesus. I take my eyes off You and panic. (You've seen me do this lots of times, I'm sure!) Then I remember that's what faith is for. It calms me down. It reminds me that I'm not the one in charge—You are. And when I remember that You're in charge, I realize I have nothing to worry about. Whew! It feels so good to remember that it's not up to me. It's *all* up to You! Amen.

─────── Think about it: ───────

If you oversaw all of the problems in your own life, you would have a lot to worry about! But with God in charge, you can rest easy. What problems do you need to give Him today?

Self-Control

*I keep working over my body. I make it obey me. I do
this because I am afraid that after I have preached the
Good News to others, I myself might be put aside.*
1 CORINTHIANS 9:27

I don't always make my body obey, Jesus. I know I should,
but I don't. Sometimes I mess up. I get tempted, and I
give in to the temptation. I eat more than I should, or I
talk bad about someone. I tell fibs, and I'm not always
kind. You want me to control my mouth, my mind, and
my heart. I'm definitely going to need Your help with
this! Tomorrow, when I wake up, please give me all the
self-control I need to make it through the day. Amen.

Think about it:

If you had no self-control, what would
happen? Why do you suppose God
cares so much about self-control?

Waiting For My Crown

*Everyone who runs in a race does many things
so his body will be strong. He does it to get a
crown that will soon be worth nothing, but we
work for a crown that will last forever.*

1 CORINTHIANS 9:25

Life is hard, and sometimes I feel like giving up, Jesus.
That's especially true some nights when I climb into
bed. I just want to pull the covers over my head and say,
"Enough!" I don't always feel like waking up the next
morning to the same crazy life. But You say that I need
to keep running the race, so I will. I'm getting stronger
and stronger, the more problems I face. And one day,
You'll give me a crown and say, "Good job! Race well
run, girl!" So I'll keep going even when I don't feel like
it. Amen.

———————— Think about it: ————————

What if Jesus hadn't finished His race? What if
He gave up before dying for your sins? Aren't
you glad He ran all the way to the finish line?

YOU KNOW MY LIMITS

You have never been tempted to sin in any different way than other people. God is faithful. He will not allow you to be tempted more than you can take. But when you are tempted, He will make a way for you to keep from falling into sin.

1 CORINTHIANS 10:13

You know me so well, Jesus. You know me inside and out. You see how I'm tempted to do things I shouldn't, but You make sure I don't have too much temptation. You always make a way out for me so that I don't end up in trouble. Thanks for looking out for me and for taking such great care of me. I'm so grateful! Amen.

--- Think about it: ---

What temptations are hardest for you? Lying? Cheating? Being mean to others? Gossiping? Anger? God can take control of your temptations and help you overcome them.

DECISIONS, DECISIONS!

Trust in the Lord with all your heart, and do not trust in your own understanding. Agree with Him in all your ways, and He will make your paths straight.
PROVERBS 3:5–6

Sometimes decisions are hard, Jesus! Deciding what to wear. What to eat. Who to be friends with. Which sports to play. Then there are the *big* decisions, like giving my heart to You. (Best decision ever!) I don't always know what to do when I'm facing decisions, but You do. That's why I lean on You. I can trust You to help me make the very best decisions. You will make my paths straight, for sure. Amen.

——————— Think about it: ———————

When you don't know what to do, who does?
How can you know you're making the right decisions?

Sometimes I Forget

But as for you, hold on to what you have learned and know to be true. Remember where you learned them.
2 Timothy 3:14

I don't always get things right, Jesus. Sometimes I mess up. (Oops!) Today, I messed up a few times. Tomorrow, I hope to do better. I've learned so much from You, and I want to do the right things, but sometimes I forget. I get so busy or so focused on myself that I totally forget what the Bible says I should do. (Sorry about that!) Tomorrow, I'll do my best to remember Your Word and then obey! Amen.

--- Think about it: ---

How good is your memory? Do you remember everything you've been taught? Of course not! Some life lessons must be repeated to sink in. But know that Jesus loves you no matter what.

Teach Me Your Ways

Teach me Your way, O Lord. I will walk in Your truth. May my heart fear Your name.
PSALM 86:11

I like to do things my way, Jesus. I usually think my way is best. But then I remember Your way is the best way. When I want to get angry, You say, "Be calm, girl!" When I want to tell a fib, You say, "The truth will set you free." When I want to do something that I know will make my parents unhappy, You say, "Honor your father and mother." Your way is always best, so keep teaching me even when I'm stubborn. I want to walk in Your truth, Jesus. Amen.

———— Think about it: ————

Who knows best—you or Jesus? Do you ever get things wrong? Does He?

TURN AROUND, GIRL

But you must be sorry for your sins and turn from them. You must turn to God and have your sins taken away. Then many times your soul will receive new strength from the Lord.
Acts 3:19

I don't always go the right way, Jesus. Sometimes I get off course. I make a wrong turn. Sometimes I do unkind things and then don't even feel bad about it. I forget that it breaks Your heart when I sin. Tomorrow, help me to take the right actions along the path You've chosen for me. And when I do mess up, please help me to turn from my sin right away. Amen.

—————— Think about it: ——————

Your journey with Jesus is like a journey down a long road. What would happen if you accidentally took a wrong turn and went the wrong way? Isn't it always best to stick close to Him?

PEER PRESSURE

*Do you think I am trying to get the favor of men,
or of God? If I were still trying to please men,
I would not be a servant owned by Christ.*
GALATIANS 1:10

It happens a lot, Jesus. I worry too much about what people think about me. I try too hard to fit in. I want to be accepted, part of the group. I don't know why I'm such a people pleaser. Your Word says that I should be a God pleaser instead. Tomorrow, please help me remember that making Your heart happy is much more important than fitting in or pleasing my friends. It's Your favor I want, Jesus. Amen.

———————— Think about it: ————————

Whose opinion matters most? Who should
you try to please—your friends or Jesus?

THE RiGHT KiND OF FRiENDS

Do not let anyone fool you. Bad people can make those who want to live good become bad. Keep your minds awake! Stop sinning. Some do not know God at all. I say this to your shame.
1 CORINTHIANS 15:33–34

I'm not always the best at picking the right friends, Jesus. Sometimes I spend too much time hanging out with the kids who don't follow You like they should. I'm learning that kids who misbehave want me to misbehave too. They want me to follow them. But I'm onto their tricks! I won't do it. I won't let anyone fool me. I'm keeping my eyes open and my mind alert to their plans. From now on, I'm picking the right kind of friends. Amen.

─────── Think about it: ───────

There are two kinds of friends—the ones who help you get closer to God and the ones who want to pull you away. Which ones should you hang out with?

Walk With Wise Ones

*He who walks with wise men will be wise, but the
one who walks with fools will be destroyed.*
PROVERBS 13:20

I'm trying to figure out what it means to be wise, Jesus. Is it the same thing as being smart, or is it something different? Some of my friends are super smart, but they don't act in wise ways. They make bad choices and hurt people. Sometimes when I hang out with them, I end up making bad choices too. I guess that's not very wise of me! Tomorrow when I wake up, help me walk in wisdom and choose friends who do that too. Amen.

———————— Think about it: ————————

Being smart and being wise—in what
ways are they different?

YOU'RE WAITING FOR ME

The Lord is not slow about keeping His promise as some people think. He is waiting for you. The Lord does not want any person to be punished forever. He wants all people to be sorry for their sins and turn from them.
2 PETER 3:9

I don't like to keep people waiting, Jesus. I don't want to be the reason we're late! It happens sometimes, but it's always embarrassing when it does. I especially don't want to keep You waiting! If You ask me to do something, I want to do it right away. You ask me to say I'm sorry right away when I've hurt someone (or hurt You), and I want to do it quickly! Please forgive me for the times I have kept You waiting. Amen.

———————— Think about it: ————————

God always keeps His promises to you.
Do you always keep your promises to Him?

YOU DO WHAT YOU SAY, JESUS

*If we tell Him our sins, He is faithful and we
can depend on Him to forgive us of our sins.
He will make our lives clean from all sin.*

1 JOHN 1:9

You don't make promises and then break them, Jesus.
I know lots of people who do that, but You *never* do.
You say that I can confess my sins to You and that You
will forgive me, just like that! And You do it every single
time. You're so faithful. I can depend on You to forgive
me no matter what I've done wrong. Show me how I
can be more dependable like You, Lord. Amen.

--------- Think about it: ---------

God wants you to tell Him your sins. Do you do
that? Do you confess them to Him? Before you
fall asleep tonight, get those icky things off your
chest, girl. Tell Him. He will forgive you right
away, and you'll have a good night's sleep.

I Will OBEY

Children, as Christians, obey your parents.
This is the right thing to do. Respect your father
and mother. This is the first Law given that had a
promise. The promise is this: If you respect your
father and mother, you will live a long time and
your life will be full of many good things.
EPHESIANS 6:1–4

The word *obey* doesn't always sound like much fun, Jesus.
I know You want me to obey my parents and teachers—
and I do try—but it's not always easy. Mom says, "Pick
up your dirty clothes off the floor," and I forget. I get
busy doing something else. But You're teaching me
that it breaks Your heart when I don't respect them,
so tomorrow I'm going to try harder. I want to bless
them—and You. Amen.

--------- Think about it: ---------

If you never obeyed your parents,
what would happen?

I Will Listen

*Listen to your father, who gave you life,
and don't despise your mother when she is old.*
PROVERBS 23:22 NLT

I'm not always the best listener, Jesus. Sometimes my parents say things to me, and it goes in one ear and out the other! I pretend like I'm paying attention, but I'm really not. I know You want me to be a better listener, so I will try, but I'm going to need Your help. The Bible says that my parents' words are important, and I need to start treating them that way. Now I know how You must feel when Your kids ignore You. It must break Your heart. I'll lean in close to listen to You—and to them. Amen.

——————— Think about it: ———————

God is the best parent of all, and His Word
is filled with wise words. Do you always
listen to those words and obey them?

THE RIGHT THING TO DO

Children, as Christians, obey your parents.
This is the right thing to do.
EPHESIANS 6:1

Sometimes I don't know the right thing from the wrong thing, Jesus. I look at a situation and say, "What should I do?" because I really don't know. But You've made one thing super-duper obvious: following what my parents say is always the right thing—every single time. I don't feel like it sometimes (just keeping it real). They ask me to do hard stuff. Inconvenient stuff. Stuff that pulls me away from my friends and fun activities. But if it means that much to You, I'll do it, Lord! Amen.

———————— Think about it: ————————

Why does God care so much that
you do what your parents say?

BROTHERS AND SISTERS

*"I give you a new Law. You are to love each other.
You must love each other as I have loved you. If you love
each other, all men will know you are My followers."*
JOHN 13:34–35

Sometimes the people who are hardest to be kind to are the ones in my own house. I'll admit it, Lord—I get cranky around my siblings now and then. They don't make my life easy! They're annoying and get in my space. They make fun of me or take my stuff. They lie about me to Mom and Dad. But You say that I need to love my siblings as much as I love myself. I'm going to need Your help with this one, Jesus! Amen.

─────────── Think about it: ───────────

God placed you in your family. Why do you
suppose He chose this one for you?

TROUBLE SHARERS

*A friend loves at all times. A brother
is born to share troubles.*
PROVERBS 17:17

When I'm really close to someone, I feel what they feel.
When my brother or sister is hurting, I hurt too. And
when a good friend is going through something hard, it's
almost like I can feel it as well, Jesus. I guess that's how
it's supposed to be when you love someone. Tomorrow,
when I wake up, please point me in the direction of the
ones who need someone to share their troubles. I want
to be the best possible friend to the ones who are going
through hard times. Amen.

—————————— Think about it: ——————————

Does Jesus help you through your troubles? How?

OOPS!

If a person says, "I love God," but hates his brother, he is a liar. If a person does not love his brother whom he has seen, how can he love God Whom he has not seen?

1 JOHN 4:20

This is a hard verse, Jesus! I tell everyone that I love You, but I don't always act like I love the people around me. I'm a hypocrite. Some of them are really, *really* hard to love! Does that make me a liar if I'm unkind to others? I don't want to be a liar! I'm going to need help from You to figure this out. Show me how to love others so that when I say, "I love Jesus!" I'm being totally truthful. Amen.

———— Think about it: ————

Why do you think Jesus says that loving others is important if you claim to love Him?

I'M SO ASHAMED SOMETIMES

*Instead of your shame you will have a share
that is twice as much. Instead of being without
honor, they will sing for joy over all you receive.
So they will have twice as much in their land,
and joy that lasts forever will be theirs.*
ISAIAH 61:7

I messed up today, Jesus, and now I'm embarrassed and ashamed. Everyone knows what I did. I feel bad because I know I did the wrong thing. Will these shameful feelings stay with me forever? Please wash them away. When I wake up in the morning, I want to start over again without these icky feelings. Please help me, Jesus. Thank You. Amen.

——————— Think about it: ———————

Jesus doesn't want you to go on feeling ashamed after you've asked Him to forgive you. So why should you let shame hold you back, girl?

A FACE LIKE HARD STONE

*For the Lord God helps Me, so I am not put
to shame. I have set My face like hard stone,
and know that I will not be ashamed.*

ISAIAH 50:7

Sometimes I have to talk myself into doing the right thing. It's like I must turn to stone to avoid the comments people throw at me. They toss fiery darts with their words, trying to embarrass me, but I let those darts bounce right off me. They don't even hurt because my eyes are fixed on You, Jesus. Those mean words can't put me to shame because I see Your eyes of love even when I mess up. Thanks for helping me avoid those ugly words. Amen.

——————— Think about it: ———————

Why do you suppose God says we should set
our faces like hard stone? Could it be that
nothing can hurt us if we're glued to Him?

FACES SHINING WITH JOY

I looked for the Lord, and He answered me. And He took away all my fears. They looked to Him and their faces shined with joy. Their faces will never be ashamed.
PSALM 34:4–5

There are some happy people out there, Jesus. I know a lot of them. Their faces are always shining with joy even when they're going through hard stuff. They come to the end of a long, hard day and still have pleasant smiles on their faces. I want to be more like that, Lord. I want my face to shine with joy even on the hard days. No matter what happens to me tomorrow, give me a smile that I can share with others. Amen.

——————— Think about it: ———————

Is joy contagious? If so, why not spread it around! You can have a face shining with joy so that others will ask, "What's your secret?"

HARD WORK

Some good comes from all work.
Nothing but talk leads only to being poor.
PROVERBS 14:23

I work hard some days, Jesus! Other days, I'm pretty lazy. I lie around on the couch or my bed, glad I don't have to go anywhere or do anything. I know that You care a lot about hard work. You don't want me to waste time. It's good to rest, but too much? That's not healthy. So when I wake up in the morning, give me the energy to get everything done that needs to be done—and all with a smile on my face. Amen.

——————— Think about it: ———————

Why does God care so much about hard work? Was He a hard worker? (Hint: He created the whole world in six days.)

All Things

I can do all things because Christ gives me the strength.
PHILIPPIANS 4:13

"*All things.*" I read those words, and right away I have doubts, Jesus. There are so many things I feel like I can't do. But I know that, with You, all things are possible. Even the hardest day is easier when I remember You're right here, walking through it with me. You give me strength when I am so weak I can hardly get out of bed. Tonight, as I rest my head on my pillow, I just want to say thank You for helping with every problem I face. Amen.

———— Think about it: ————

Can you think of a time when Jesus
gave you strength in place of weakness?
How did it change your outlook?

I Will Give It to You

Trust your work to the Lord, and your plans will work out well.

PROVERBS 16:3

Sometimes I forget who I'm working for, Jesus. I think that all my hard work is for me, myself, and I. I set goals, and I'm excited about reaching them. (Yay!) Then I remember that all the work I do in this lifetime is really meant to bring glory to You, not myself. It's all for You. My plans are going to work out great as long as I focus on You. So tomorrow, I'm going to work hard—not for me, but for You, Jesus! Amen.

———————— Think about it: ————————

You have big plans, and you work hard to reach those goals, girl, but who are you working for—yourself or Jesus?

YOU ARE NEAR

The Lord is near to those who have a broken heart.
And He saves those who are broken in spirit.
PSALM 34:18

Sometimes when I get really sad, I feel like no one knows or cares, Jesus. It feels so lonely to be in that place. Then I remember that Your Word says You are near to those who have a broken heart. I'm so glad You're sticking close by me during the hard times, because You give me courage and strength to face the hard stuff. Show me how I can help other people who are feeling sad and lonely too, Lord. I want to be more like You. Amen.

—————— Think about it: ——————

If Jesus cares for people who are sad and lonely, doesn't it make sense that He wants you to care for them too?

BYE, BYE TROUBLES!

"Do not let not your hearts be troubled.
You believe in God; believe also in me."
JOHN 14:1 NIV

Sometimes I hang on to my troubles, Jesus. Today, I had some rough patches, and instead of getting past them, I made an even bigger deal out of them. That's not Your way, is it? You want me to give my troubles to You—to let go of them and watch as You take care of them for me. Tomorrow, I plan to do that! I believe what You say. You really are my "trouble taker"! Thank You so much for caring for me. Amen.

——————— Think about it: ———————

Why do you suppose Jesus doesn't want you to hang on to your troubles? What would happen if you were angry or upset every single day of your life?

Cast It Away

Cast your cares on the LORD, and he will sustain
you; he will never let the righteous be shaken.
PSALM 55:22 NIV

I know what it means to cast something, Jesus. It's like when you're fishing and you cast the line into the water, far away from yourself. That's what You want me to do with my troubles. You don't want me to hang on to them. I'm supposed to let go. Today, I forgot to let go of some of my troubles, but I'm doing that right now! I'm casting them into the sea of forgetfulness and starting over fresh tomorrow! Amen.

——————— Think about it: ———————

Have you ever been fishing? Have you ever cast your line into the water? Why do you suppose God uses this same idea when He talks about getting rid of your burdens?

I Will Follow What You Say

*Obey the Word of God. If you hear only and
do not act, you are only fooling yourself.*
JAMES 1:22

Some days, I'm guilty of not following You, Jesus. I know what Your Word says, but I have ideas of my own. I follow after those popular girls who don't always do or say the right thing. I want to fit in, so I push aside Your Word. Please forgive me for that! I'm only fooling myself if I pretend. You want me to read Your Word and then do what it says. Fresh start tomorrow, please! I'd like another chance to get this right. Amen.

—————— Think about it: ——————

What good would it do you to read God's Word
but not follow it? You should try to do your
best, girl. Read the Word—and then follow it!

Little Tongue, Big Problem

*The tongue is also a small part of the body,
but it can speak big things. See how a very
small fire can set many trees on fire.*

JAMES 3:5

My tongue gets me in trouble a lot, Jesus. I know You know this. You see and hear everything. I don't mean to smart off to my mom. I don't mean to say ugly things to my brother. I don't mean to sass my elders, but sometimes I mess up and do it anyway. You say that the tongue is small but fierce! It can set things on fire. I've seen that a time or two. I've started a few fiery troubles with the words from my mouth. Please forgive me and help me start over. Amen.

—————— Think about it: ——————

Why do you suppose God compares
the tongue to a fire?

BLESSING AND CURSING

Giving thanks and speaking bad words come from the same mouth. My Christian brothers, this is not right! Does a well of water give good water and bad water from the same place?

JAMES 3:10–11

Oops! I did it again. The same mouth that speaks praises and blessings just slipped up and said something bad. You say in Your Word that I shouldn't let blessing and cursing come from the same mouth. I need to back away from the harsh, ugly words and speak only kind, loving ones. A well doesn't give both good water and bad. And my mouth shouldn't give good speech and bad either. Help me, please. I want to do better. Amen.

—————— Think about it: ——————

How is your mouth like a well of water?

LOVE ISN'T JEALOUS

Love does not give up. Love is kind. Love is not jealous. Love does not put itself up as being important. Love has no pride.
1 CORINTHIANS 13:4

I always say that I love others, Jesus, but sometimes I don't act like it. I get cranky. I demand my own way. And some days, I get jealous. When my friend gets a new smartphone and I don't. When my brother gets a new toy. When my classmate gets a new outfit or the shoes I've been wanting. I want what they have. (Just keeping it real!) But Your Word says that love isn't jealous. It doesn't crave what others have. Help me put jealousy away and want only You, Jesus. Amen.

——————— Think about it: ———————

Why is jealousy such a big deal? Why does Jesus want you to stay away from it?

Jealousy Has a Bad Ending

*Wherever you find jealousy and fighting, there will
be trouble and every other kind of wrong-doing.*
JAMES 3:16

I read a lot of books, and some don't have great endings,
Jesus. I wish they would end differently. That's kind of
how it is when people get jealous. Their story doesn't
end well. Instead of a happy ending, they end up fighting
and arguing. You say to stay away from envy, or jealousy,
so that my story ends well. I'm doing my best, but I'll
need Your help for sure. Amen.

——————— Think about it: ———————

Do you ever think about how your story
will end? What if you put away jealousy
and spend your time loving others?

I Will Stop Pretending

*Put out of your life hate and lying. Do not
pretend to be someone you are not. Do not
always want something someone else has.
Do not say bad things about other people.*

1 PETER 2:1

Some people say, "Fake it till you make it." But I'm not
wired that way, Jesus! I'm done with faking it. I'm done
with pretending to be something—or someone—I'm not.
It's not worth it. I'm just going to be me—the me You
made me to be. I'll stop pretending to be something
else just so I can fit in. Help me be the very best me I
can be, Lord. Amen.

——————— Think about it: ———————

Why did God make you, you? You're not
meant to be like anyone else, girl!

BFFS

A man who has friends must be a friend, but there is a friend who stays nearer than a brother.
PROVERBS 18:24

There are lots of people to be friends with, but I really love having close friends, Jesus. Those are the ones I can talk to when I'm having a hard day or need a quiet conversation. I'm happy that You've given me friends, but I'm super happy that You're my BFF—my very best friend of all. I can tell You anything and everything. I know that You're always listening and that You care. Thanks for being such a great friend! Amen.

─────── Think about it: ───────

Jesus is a friend who sticks closer than a brother (Proverbs 18:24). He's part of your family and wants you to know that you can trust Him with all your struggles. What makes Him so trustworthy?

IRON SHARPENS IRON

*Iron is made sharp with iron, and one
man is made sharp by a friend.*
PROVERBS 27:17

I'm starting to get it, Jesus! We become more like the
people we hang out with. When I hang out with not-
so-great people, they rub off on me. When I hang out
with people who love You, I become more like them. I
get "sharper" in my faith when I spend time with them.
Please show me the very best people I should be hanging
out with. I want to be a good witness to everyone, but
I want to learn from the very best! Amen.

——————————— Think about it: ———————————

How does spending time with faith-filled
people help you grow in your faith?

TWO ARE BETTER THAN ONE

Two are better than one, because they have
good pay for their work. For if one of them falls,
the other can help him up. But it is hard for the
one who falls when there is no one to lift him up.
ECCLESIASTES 4:9–10

When I'm going through something hard, it helps to have people around me. I'm so glad You've given me a family and friends, Jesus. If I fall down, they lift me up. If they fall down, I lift them up. We help each other because we care. I know You care too. You're the best friend any of us could have. We could never make it through the hard times without You. Thanks for surrounding me with love. Amen.

———————— Think about it: ————————

When you're going through a hard time,
would you rather be alone or with someone
else? Two are always better than one!

Before the Day Is Done

If you are angry, do not let it become sin.
Get over your anger before the day is finished.
Ephesians 4:26

Temper, temper! Some days, I have a terrible temper,
Lord. I get to the end of the day and am ready to crawl
into bed, but I'm still mad about something that happened hours before. Your Word says I shouldn't go
to bed angry. I need to get rid of my anger before it
becomes sin. So, right here and right now, I ask You to
forgive me for my temper. I give it all to You so I can
have a good night's sleep and wake up in a much better
mood. Amen.

——————— Think about it: ———————

Why does Jesus want you to get rid of
anger before you get into bed? Can't
you just deal with it in the morning?

S-L-O-W DOWN!

He who is slow to get angry has great understanding, but he who has a quick temper makes his foolish way look right.

PROVERBS 14:29

I move really fast sometimes! A friend says something mean to me, and I say something mean right back—super-duper fast! I don't even stop to think about it. The words just come rushing out of my mouth. You want me to slow down, Jesus. You say, "Don't be foolish, girl!" You want me to pause and think about what I'm going to say before I say it. Tomorrow, I will do my best—with Your help. Amen.

——————— Think about it: ———————

Are you a fast-moving girl? Do you often speak without thinking first? Why does Jesus want you to s-l-o-w down and think about your words before they come out of your mouth?

RiGHt WitH YOU

A man's anger does not allow him to be right with God.
JAMES 1:20

I don't like that icky feeling when my relationship is "off" with someone, Jesus. That feeling I have when my best friend isn't speaking to me. That horrible feeling I have when Mom is mad at me. Things are always better when I'm right with others. The same is true of my relationship with You. I want to be right with You, but when I'm angry and have a temper, that separates me from You. It's like I'm saying, "Leave me alone, Jesus! I just want to be mad right now!" I know You understand those times, but You want me to get rid of my anger and be close to You. Help me, Lord. Amen.

———— Think about it: ————

Anger is the great separator. It divides people, and it also brings division between you and God. What happens when you're separated from those you love?

SMILING THROUGH THE BAD TIMES

*My Christian brothers, you should be happy
when you have all kinds of tests. You know these
prove your faith. It helps you not to give up.*

JAMES 1:2–3

It's weird, Jesus! Most people get really upset when they go through hard times, but the Bible says bad times should bring a smile to my face. (Really?) You are teaching me some great lessons in the middle of the hard stuff, so I'll do my best to keep smiling and keep going no matter how difficult things get. I know that others are watching me, and they are going to say, "How do you do that? How can you smile when you're going through something hard?" And I will answer with one word: "Jesus!" Amen.

——————— Think about it: ———————

When you respond to hard things with a positive attitude, how does it impact those around you?

I'M ASKING JESUS!

If you do not have wisdom, ask God for it.
He is always ready to give it to you and will
never say you are wrong for asking.
JAMES 1:5

It feels like I'm always asking for stuff, Jesus. At Christmas, my list is pretty long. For my birthday? Yeah, I have a list then too! I'm always asking my parents or grandparents for stuff. Sometimes I forget that I can come to You to ask for the important things—like wisdom. When I ask, You're quick to give me what I need. And I'm learning that what I want and what I need are two different things. Thank You for loving me enough to give me the important stuff. Amen.

————————— Think about it: —————————

Would you consider yourself needy? Are you always asking for stuff? Who do you bug the most? Why not take those requests to God instead?

NO WAVES

You must have faith as you ask Him.
You must not doubt. Anyone who doubts is like
a wave which is pushed around by the sea.
JAMES 1:6

Your Word says that a person who doesn't have faith is like a wave knocked around by the sea. Wow. Waves can be pretty strong. I've been in some wavy water before, and it almost knocked me off my feet. I guess I'd better keep my faith strong so I don't topple over. Thank You for reminding me that my faith matters. A little bit of it goes a long way. It will keep me on my feet when life is hard. I won't doubt You, Lord. I will trust. Amen.

———————— Think about it: ————————

Why does God compare doubt to a wave?
What happened the last time you doubted God?

LISTEN MUCH, SPEAK LITTLE

*My Christian brothers, you know everyone
should listen much and speak little.
He should be slow to become angry.*
JAMES 1:19

Uh-oh! This is a tough one, Jesus. I don't always listen.
I'm usually too busy trying to get my point across. I
want people to understand how I feel. But sometimes
it's better if I keep my lips closed and my ears open.
Other people have important things to say too. I don't
want to miss anything because I'm so busy blabbering
on. I need Your help, Lord! Amen.

——————————— Think about it: ———————————

God gave you two ears and only one mouth.
Why do you suppose that is? Could it be that
He wants you to listen more and speak less?

NEEDING NOTHING

*Learn well how to wait so you will be strong
and complete and in need of nothing.*

JAMES 1:4

I'm always telling people about all the things I need. "I need new shoes." "I need a cheeseburger." "I need a puppy." "I need more friends." The list goes on and on. You've seen it, Jesus. I even tell You my needs. I'm excited that You see what my real needs are, and You make sure I always have what I need. Sometimes I have to wait awhile, but You always come through. That makes me very, very happy. Amen.

——————— Think about it: ———————

Has God ever let you down? Do you have enough food to eat? Are you wearing clothes? Do you have shoes on your feet? He's got you covered, girl!

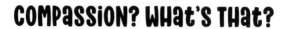

COMPASSION? WHAT'S THAT?

Therefore, as God's chosen people, holy and dearly loved, clothe yourselves with compassion, kindness, humility, gentleness and patience. Bear with each other and forgive one another if any of you has a grievance against someone. Forgive as the Lord forgave you.

COLOSSIANS 3:12–13 NIV

I don't know much about this word *compassion*, Jesus. What does it mean, exactly? If I'm compassionate toward someone, does that mean I feel sorry for them? Or does it just mean I care? I care about lots of people. I feel sad when they go through hard times. That's because I love them so much. Thanks for making me care. Amen.

——————— Think about it: ———————

Being compassionate means that you notice and care about what others are going through. Do you have a compassionate heart?

LOVE WITH A KIND HEART

*Last of all, you must share the same thoughts
and the same feelings. Love each other with a
kind heart and with a mind that has no pride.*

1 PETER 3:8

You want me to love with a kind heart, don't You, Jesus?
But here's the thing: some people are easier to love
than others. I'll be honest—some people are very, very
hard to be kind to. They're mean to me, and they say
horrible things. But You want me to love even the most
unlovable. I want to care as You care and love as You
love, but I'm going to need Your help! Amen.

─────────── Think about it: ───────────

Why would Jesus ask you to love the unlovable?
Who else is going to love them if you don't?

COMFORT IN OUR TROUBLES

*He gives us comfort in all our troubles. Then we can
comfort other people who have the same troubles.
We give the same kind of comfort God gives us.*

2 CORINTHIANS 1:4

Loving You is like having a big, cozy blanket, Jesus. You comfort me when I'm feeling down in the dumps. I don't always like to tell other people when I'm feeling icky, but I can tell You. You always understand. And best of all, You care—which is why You wrap me in that cozy blanket of Your love. Now that I understand how much You love me, it's easier to share that love with others. I can give the same comfort You've given me. Thanks for teaching me that! Amen.

—————— Think about it: ——————

If a baby was never soothed or comforted
by its mother, what would happen? In some
ways you're like a tiny babe—and God always
wraps you in His arms when you're hurting.

A GIRL WHO FINISHES WELL

*I have fought a good fight. I have finished the
work I was to do. I have kept the faith.*

2 TIMOTHY 4:7

I want to be a girl who finishes well, Jesus. Sometimes
I start stuff—like a good book or a puzzle—and I give
up before finishing. Other times I start working on a
homework assignment but get distracted. And sometimes (just being honest), I start cleaning my room but
give up before I get it tidied. (Hey, there's a lot of cool
stuff in my room to distract me!) You care as much
about my finishes as my starts, so help me do better
tomorrow. Amen.

—————— Think about it: ——————

What if God had started creating the world,
only to get distracted when He got to the
aardvarks? He finishes well, and you should too!

I Will Keep Running

All these many people who have had faith in God are around us like a cloud. Let us put every thing out of our lives that keeps us from doing what we should. Let us keep running in the race that God has planned for us.

HEBREWS 12:1

I get so tired sometimes, Jesus! I'm a girl who's always on the go! School. Friends. Family stuff. Church. Sports. Some nights, I climb into bed so exhausted I wonder if I can keep going. But You tell me I can, and I should! So I'll keep running the race no matter how hard it might seem. I want to be like the great men and women of the Bible who ran their race all the way to the very end! Amen.

——————— Think about it: ———————

What if Noah hadn't built the ark? What if Moses hadn't led the Israelites to the promised land?

A HeaVenly PRIze

I press on to reach the end of the race and receive the heavenly prize for which God, through Christ Jesus, is calling us.

PHILIPPIANS 3:14 NLT

I'm still going, going, going, Jesus! I haven't given up, even on days when my workload is huge! Your Word tells me that I'm going to get a heavenly prize if I keep doing the things You've called me to do. I can't wait to see what heaven looks like! I've heard it has streets of gold and pearly gates. I've heard there are mansions there. Wow! It's going to be a prize like no other, and I can't wait to see it for myself. Thanks for the promise of heaven. Amen.

Think about it:

There's always a prize for the person who wins a race, right? God has an even bigger prize waiting for you in heaven. What do you think heaven will be like?

BODY IMAGE

I will give thanks to You, for the greatness of the way I was made brings fear. Your works are great and my soul knows it very well.

PSALM 139:14

Sometimes I look in the mirror and don't like what I see, Jesus. Sometimes I don't like my hair. Or my freckles. Or my big feet. I moan and groan about how I wish I could look like some of the other girls. Then I remember that You created me just as I am, and You think I'm amazing! Tonight, please give me sweet dreams, and help me remember that what I look like on the outside isn't important to You. It's what's on the inside that counts. Amen.

Think about it:

Who created you to look like you do? If God made those decisions—about your hair, skin, size, and shape—who are you to argue with Him? Learn to love yourself as He loves you.

A Beautiful Heart

*Your beauty should come from the inside. It should come
from the heart. This is the kind that lasts. Your beauty
should be a gentle and quiet spirit. In God's sight this
is of great worth and no amount of money can buy it.*

1 PETER 3:4

Some girls are really pretty on the outside, but their
hearts are ugly! (I know a few like that!) They get a
lot of attention because of their looks, but the way
they treat others isn't so pretty. They're mean and say
ugly things about people behind their backs. Your Word
says that my beauty needs to come from my heart. If
I'm kind and loving to people, I'll be beautiful in Your
eyes, Lord. I want to be the prettiest girl I can be—from
the inside out! Thanks for reminding me how! Amen.

—————— Think about it: ——————

What good would it do you if you were beautiful
on the outside but treated people in an ugly way?

BEAUTY FROM LOVING YOU

Pleasing ways lie and beauty comes to nothing,
but a woman who fears the Lord will be praised.
PROVERBS 31:30

Not everyone is a beauty queen. Not everyone is gorgeous on the outside. I know lots of people who are wonderful Christians—loving and kind to all—and they look beautiful to me because I see straight to their hearts. I'm learning that a girl who loves Jesus is truly beautiful no matter her physical appearance because of the love in her heart for You. You radiate beauty, and it spills over onto everyone who loves You back. I do love You, Jesus. I really, really do! Amen.

——————— Think about it: ———————

Jesus loves you so much! Why do you suppose
it's so important to love Him back? Why would
He care whether you loved Him or not?

Me, Myself, and Pride

*Pride comes before being destroyed and
a proud spirit comes before a fall.*
PROVERBS 16:18

I get a little prideful sometimes, Jesus. I like to brag on myself. When I accomplish something great—like getting a good grade on my report card or getting a good score in a sporting competition—I tell everyone about it. I get a little puffed up as I brag, brag, brag. You tell me to be careful, not to let my pride get too big! People who make a big deal out of how great they think they are usually end up looking foolish in the end. So I'll watch my pride. I promise! Amen.

——————— Think about it: ———————

Do you have feelings of pride you need
to get rid of? Ask God for help. Make
tomorrow about others, not yourself.

MORE LOVING-FAVOR

But He gives us more loving-favor. For the Holy Writings say, "God works against the proud but gives loving-favor to those who have no pride."

JAMES 4:6

There are days when I don't feel like I deserve Your goodness, but You pour it out anyway, Jesus. That's one reason I'm going to work hard not to brag on myself too much. Your Word says that You give Your loving-favor to those who have no pride. (Some days I mess up, but You love me anyway.) If I get rid of my pride, then You'll bless me even more than You already do, so I'm doing my best to get rid of that icky bragging! Thanks for Your help with this, Lord! Amen.

————————— Think about it: —————————

What is God's favor? And why is it such a special gift?

BROKEN HEARTS MENDED

*He heals those who have a broken
heart. He heals their sorrows.*

PSALM 147:3

I have had days when my heart felt like it was broken, Jesus. I couldn't stop crying because it hurt so much. Sometimes people say mean things and hurt my feelings. Sometimes I go through hard times when life seems unfair. But even in the middle of my brokenness, You reach down and wrap me in Your loving arms. You care very deeply about the things that break my heart, and You promise to mend the broken places. Thank You so much for caring about me! Amen.

——————— Think about it: ———————

If God never mended broken hearts, what would happen? Have you ever watched someone else go through a long season of brokenness?

I WON'T BE ANXIOUS

Do not be anxious about anything, but in every situation, by prayer and petition, with thanksgiving, present your requests to God. And the peace of God, which transcends all understanding, will guard your hearts and your minds in Christ Jesus.

PHILIPPIANS 4:6–7 NIV

I get pretty wound up and anxious sometimes, Jesus. It starts with a little bit of worry. Then, before I know it, I'm all twisted up with fear and anxiety. I worry about stuff I should give to You. Your Word says I shouldn't be anxious about anything. Wow! That's a lot of stuff I should be giving to You instead of fretting over. So today, as this day comes to an end, I give the worries and anxieties of the day to You. Tomorrow is a fresh new day. Please fill it with Your peace and guard my heart, I pray. Amen.

—————— Think about it: ——————

If you give your anxiety to God,
don't try to take it back, girl!

Happy with What I Have

*Keep your lives free from the love of money.
Be happy with what you have. God has said,
"I will never leave you or let you be alone." So
we can say for sure, "The Lord is my Helper. I am
not afraid of anything man can do to me."*

Hebrews 13:5–6

I want a lot. I'm always asking for stuff, Jesus. New stuff, cool stuff—lots of stuff. It's not that I need all that stuff. I'm just never really satisfied with what I have. But Your Word says I should be satisfied. I'm not supposed to be in love with money or the stuff it can buy. I know that You have me covered. I'll never want for anything. So help me put away the desire to have more, more, more. What I have is plenty! And did I mention how grateful I am for all You've given me? Thanks so much, Jesus! Amen.

———— Think about it: ————

The things you want—are they critical? Can you live without them? Are there better ways that money could be spent? Just something to think about, girl!

I'M NEVER ALONE

"I will not leave you without help as children without parents. I will come to you."
John 14:18

You promised You would never leave me, Jesus. I'm counting on that! There are times when it feels like people have abandoned me. They're not always there when I need them. I go through hard times, and sometimes I feel alone. But You said You won't leave me helpless, so I'm going to trust more in You and not spend so much time worrying about the people who don't seem to notice when I'm hurting. Thank You for loving me so much, Lord. Amen.

—————— Think about it: ——————

God created the whole wide world!
He sees everything and everyone.
Do you really think He would
forget about you? Of course not!
You're His precious child!

YOUR RIGHT HAND

*"Do not fear, for I am with you. Do not be afraid,
for I am your God. I will give you strength,
and for sure I will help you. Yes, I will hold you up
with My right hand that is right and good."*

ISAIAH 41:10

This is so cool, Jesus! Today's verse reminds me that You are holding me up with Your right hand. It's so awesome to think that You're *that* close! Your hand is holding me—when I'm making big decisions, when I'm going through a hard time, even when I'm asleep! That's how much You love me. You also promise to give me strength, and I'm so glad for that promise! Thanks for loving me so much, Lord! Amen.

—————— Think about it: ——————

How far away is God at this very moment? Hint: He's never far away! He sticks close to You always!

I WON'T SHAKE WITH FEAR

"Be strong and have strength of heart. Do not be afraid or shake with fear because of them. For the Lord your God is the One Who goes with you. He will be faithful to you. He will not leave you alone."

DEUTERONOMY 31:6

When I was little, I used to be afraid of the dark. It was scary to get into bed sometimes! Now, I know that You're always watching over me—in the daylight and the nighttime too. Whew! What a relief! No matter what I'm facing, You tell me that I can be strong. It's not my strength—it's Yours! Even when I'm feeling my weakest, You breathe strength into me! So I won't shake or tremble, Jesus. I'll stick close to You. Amen.

Think about it:

Is Jesus saying that you must be strong, or is He saying that He's strong enough to handle all you're going through?

I'M NOT LIKE EVERYONE ELSE

We all have different gifts that God has given to us by His loving-favor. We are to use them. If someone has the gift of preaching the Good News, he should preach. He should use the faith God has given him.
ROMANS 12:6

I'm not like everyone else, Jesus, and that's okay! I don't want to be a cookie-cutter girl! It's all right with me that I'm different. You gave me different dreams, different gifts, different opinions, even different looks! I'm unique. You planned it that way on purpose. (The world would be pretty boring if everyone looked the same and had the same talents.) Thanks for making me unique. I promise to be the best me I can be! Amen.

—————— Think about it: ——————

Why do you suppose God made everyone unique? Why don't all human beings look the same? God is very creative, isn't He?

HELP EACH OTHER

God has given each of you a gift. Use it to help each other. This will show God's loving-favor.
1 PETER 4:10

I love to help other people, Jesus. And I'm so glad You've given me gifts so that I can do that. You've given me the gift of love. I use it all the time! You've given me the gift of joy. I love to share that with others! You've given me the gift of kindness. That's a great one for helping people who are hurting. And You've given me the gift of patience. I can help my friends and family by using more of that. Everything You've given me is really a blessing—not just for me, but for those I love too. I'm grateful! Amen.

––––––––– Think about it: –––––––––

How can you help a loved one by sharing the gift of joy? How can you help by showing kindness?

I AM A LiGHT

"You are the light of the world. You cannot hide a city that is on a mountain. Men do not light a lamp and put it under a basket. They put it on a table so it gives light to all in the house. Let your light shine in front of men. Then they will see the good things you do and will honor your Father Who is in heaven."
MATTHEW 5:14–16

When I gave my heart to You, You placed Your light in me, Jesus. Now, You want me to shine for everyone to see. I will do my best to be a good witness for You so that other people can come to know You. When they do, You will turn on the light inside of them too! Before long, the whole world will be shining bright for You! Amen.

——————— Think about it: ———————

What if you didn't shine your light? Would others know about Jesus? It's time to shine bright, girl!

What Will I Be?

Christ gave gifts to men. He gave to some the gift to be missionaries, some to be preachers, others to be preachers who go from town to town. He gave others the gift to be church leaders and teachers. These gifts help His people work well for Him.

EPHESIANS 4:11–12

It's fun to think about what I'll be when I grow up, Jesus. Will I be a teacher? A mom? An astronaut? Will I work on computers? Own a farm? Play sports? I have all sorts of dreams, but it's really up to You. For sure, You have placed gifts inside of me, and I know You will help me use them no matter my age. These gifts are meant to bless the world, whether I'm young or old. Thanks for Your great gifts! Amen.

——————— Think about it: ———————

Does God already know what you're going to be when you grow up?

I WON't TURN AWAY

The love of money is the beginning of all kinds of sin. Some people have turned from the faith because of their love for money. They have made much pain for themselves because of this.
1 TIMOTHY 6:10

This is a sad verse, Jesus. Some people get so excited about money that they turn away from their faith. I won't ever let that happen! I won't chase after money or riches. I'll just chase after You. I know that chasing after money is a bad idea, anyway, because You have already promised that You're going to take care of me no matter what. So I'll go on trusting You and never turn away! Amen.

—————— Think about it: ——————

Why do you suppose some people turn away from their faith to chase after money?

THINGS DON'T BRING LIFE

Then Jesus said to them all, "Watch yourselves!
Keep from wanting all kinds of things you
should not have. A man's life is not made up
of things, even if he has many riches."
LUKE 12:15

I look around my bedroom and see lots of things, Jesus. I see my bed, my covers, even the pajamas I'm wearing! I see a dresser with clothes in the drawer. I see a closet with stuff jammed inside. I see my shoes and my other possessions. I'm surrounded by stuff! But You have reminded me with this verse that "stuff" isn't what makes life great. Loving You and loving people (my family and friends) is really where I find life. Amen.

——————— Think about it: ———————

Why did Jesus remind us that life isn't made
up of stuff? After all, we have a lot of it! What
do you think He's trying to teach us?

CLIQUES

*Christian brothers, I ask you with all my heart in
the name of the Lord Jesus Christ to agree among
yourselves. Do not be divided into little groups.
Think and act as if you all had the same mind.*

1 CORINTHIANS 1:10

Clickety-clique-clique-clique! It feels like everyone's in
a clique these days, Jesus! They have their own little
groups, and they don't let others in. I confess that
I've been a little cliquish sometimes too. It's hard to
remember to include others when I'm so comfortable
around my friend group. But You don't want us to be
divided. It makes You happy when we include others.
So, tomorrow, remind me to invite others in. I don't
want to leave anyone out. Amen.

―――――― Think about it: ――――――

If the whole world was divided into
groups, what would happen?

NO Favorites!

My Christian brothers, our Lord Jesus Christ is the Lord of shining-greatness. Since your trust is in Him, do not look on one person as more important than another.

JAMES 2:1

Sometimes I play favorites. I don't realize I'm doing it until someone else points it out. But I hang out with one friend and ignore the others. Or I spend time with one sister but not the other. It's easy to do, Jesus! I'm naturally drawn to some people. But I'm glad You reminded me that I need to work harder to include others so that they don't feel "less than." You never make me feel "less than," and I don't want to make others feel that way either. Thanks for reminding me. Amen.

—————— Think about it: ——————

Have you ever been in a situation where someone left you out? How did it make you feel?

I Will Forgive

"When you stand to pray, if you have anything against anyone, forgive him. Then your Father in heaven will forgive your sins also."
MARK 11:25

I'm not always very quick to forgive others, Jesus. Sometimes I get hurt and hold on to that hurt for hours or even days. I have a hard time letting go. But Your Word says that I should forgive others so that You will forgive me. I don't want anything to get in the way of my relationship with You, so tonight, before I go to sleep, I'm going to do my best to forgive the ones who have hurt me—even if they never asked for my forgiveness. It's the right thing to do. Amen.

──────── Think about it: ────────

When you don't forgive someone who has hurt you, what are the consequences?

GETTING GLAD ABOUT THE BAD

We are glad for our troubles also. We know that troubles help us learn not to give up.
ROMANS 5:3

Seasons of sadness are hard to take, Jesus. I always want to be happy. No tears for me! But sometimes I can't help myself. Bad things happen, and before I know it, I'm upset. That's why I find it so interesting that You say I should be glad for my troubles. That seems strange. How can I be glad about the bad? Still, I will give it a shot. This is Your way, after all, and I want to do things Your way. I will learn, learn, learn from what I'm going through. Teach me all the lessons I need for life, Lord. Amen.

——————— Think about it: ———————

What have you learned from the bad experiences in your life? For sure you've learned not to give up! Good going, girl!

HOW MANY TIMES?

Then Peter came to Jesus and said, "Lord, how many times may my brother sin against me and I forgive him, up to seven times?" Jesus said to him, "I tell you, not seven times but seventy times seven!"
MATTHEW 18:21–22

It's not enough for me to forgive someone once, is it, Jesus? The Bible says I have to forgive over and over and over again. This isn't easy! (I guess You already know that.) Some people are mean to me—a lot. And I forgive a lot. I'll go on forgiving and trust You to take control of the mean person's heart. Just because I forgive doesn't mean I have to be BFFs with them, after all. Thanks for forgiving me over and over, by the way. Amen.

——————— Think about it: ———————

It might seem like a lot for God to expect you to forgive someone more than once, but how many times has He forgiven you?

PUT OUT THE FIRE!

When there is no wood, the fire goes out. Where there is no one telling secret stories about people, arguing stops.
PROVERBS 26:20

It's so hard not to get caught up in juicy gossip, Jesus! I feel like I'm just one person in a long line of people passing the story along. And it grows and grows. The more people know, the bigger the tale! I like this verse from Proverbs because it reminds me that gossip can stop with me. If I refuse to pass the tale on to someone else, then it comes to an end. Please remind me when I'm hearing some juicy gossip that it's not my story to share. Let it end with me! Amen.

―――――――― Think about it: ――――――――

If you saw a forest fire, would you put water on it or gasoline? Water, of course! Gossip is like that. Cover it with water, not gasoline!

I Will Watch My Talk

Watch your talk! No bad words should be coming from your mouth. Say what is good. Your words should help others grow as Christians.
EPHESIANS 4:29

I wonder what it would be like to read back over all my words at the end of the day, Lord. Even now, I'm thinking of some of the things I said today. They wouldn't make a very good book. Some words were silly. Some were angry. Some were frustrated. I didn't always bring honor to You with the things that came out of my mouth. Tomorrow, I will watch my mouth. I'll make sure bad stuff doesn't come out of it. I'll only say what's good so that I can honor You. Amen.

——————— Think about it: ———————

If you never guarded your words, what would happen over time? Would your words get sweeter or worse with time?

I WON'T HURT OTHERS

He who goes about talking to hurt people makes secrets known. So do not be with those who talk about others.
PROVERBS 20:19

Words are like weapons, aren't they, Jesus? Sometimes I shoot them like an arrow out of a bow. My goal is to hurt people with the words I say. (I'm embarrassed even to admit this, but You already know, anyway.) You don't want me to use my words as weapons. Every word out of my mouth should bring life and peace to my friends, family members, teachers, and even strangers. I won't spread gossip, and I won't deliberately hurt others with my words. Please help me with this. Amen.

—————— Think about it: ——————

Why is it important to think before you speak? What would happen if you just blurted out everything that came to mind?

I WON't JUDge

"Do not say what is wrong in other people's lives. Then other people will not say what is wrong in your life. Do not say someone is guilty. Then other people will not say you are guilty. Forgive other people and other people will forgive you."

LUKE 6:37

I get a little bit judgmental at times, Lord. I see the mistakes that others make, and I want to correct them. But You say it's not my place to try to fix the messes my friends and family members make. You will help them do better next time. If I'm too quick to point out every little flaw, they will probably start judging me too. And that doesn't feel good. Instead, I'll just forgive and pray and leave it all up to You. Amen.

——————— Think about it: ———————

Why is God the only one who should judge people? Is it because He's the only one who can see into their hearts?

LOVE, NOT HATE

Hate starts fights, but love covers all sins.
PROVERBS 10:12

When a friend or sibling hurts my feelings, I have two choices, Jesus: I can choose to love them anyway or to get angry and let hurt grow up in my heart. Sometimes it's tempting to get angry, but then after a while we're not speaking anymore. That's awkward and painful. That's why Your Word says that I should tear down walls of hate and offer love as a remedy for the pain of hurt feelings. Love is like an ocean wave. It washes over the not-so-great situation and makes everything good again. Next time, I'll offer love. Amen.

──────── Think about it: ────────

If hate builds a wall between you and the person who hurt you, what does love do?

YOU'VE LOVED ME A LONG TIME

Even before the world was made, God chose us for Himself because of His love. He planned that we should be holy and without blame as He sees us.

EPHESIANS 1:4

This scripture verse is so cool, Jesus! You knew who I was even before the world was created. How is that even possible? I wasn't born yet! I didn't have a name. I had no hair or eyes or freckles. And yet, somehow, You knew and loved me. That tells me You always had a plan for my life, even before my mother had me. My heart is happy to know that You've always known me best of all. Amen.

——————— Think about it: ———————

How long have you known your family members? How long have you known your friends? Jesus has known you much, much longer than that!

YOUR BLOOD

Because of the blood of Christ, we are bought and made free from the punishment of sin. And because of His blood, our sins are forgiven. His loving-favor to us is so rich.
EPHESIANS 1:7

I never used to understand what people were talking about when they said things like "the blood of Jesus." It made no sense to me. What blood? Where? Now I know that You died on the cross for me. When they beat You with whips, Your back bled. When You were hanging on the cross, they put a spear in Your side and blood and water spilled out. They pressed a crown of thorns on Your head, and that bled too. Now I understand that it's through Your blood that I am saved. So I thank You for giving Your life for me! Amen.

——————— Think about it: ———————

If Jesus hadn't gone to the cross and spilled His blood, how would things be different?

secret wisdom

*I pray that the great God and Father of our Lord
Jesus Christ may give you the wisdom of His
Spirit. Then you will be able to understand the
secrets about Him as you know Him better.*

EPHESIANS 1:17

Tonight, as I fall asleep, I want to ask for something special, Jesus. I don't need any new toys or clothes. I don't need anything I can see or touch. What I really need—what I really want—is to be more like You. Give me Your wisdom, I pray. Help me make wise choices and decisions. Fill me with Your Spirit so I can understand the deep secrets about You. Help me know and love You more. Amen.

———— Think about it: ————

Would you consider yourself wise?
What would happen if you never got any
wiser? It's time to grow in Him, girl!

THAT POWER IS IN ME

I pray that you will know how great [God's] power is for those who have put their trust in Him. It is the same power that raised Christ from the dead. This same power put Christ at God's right side in heaven.
EPHESIANS 1:19–20

Some days, I feel like such a weakling. I don't have the energy to tackle my problems or my chores. I just feel blah. Then I am reminded of this verse. You say that the same power that raised Jesus from the dead lives inside of me. Whoa! That's a lot of power! You've given it to me as a gift but also so that I can lead others to You. Help me as I share the good news of what You've done in my life. Thank You for Your power! Amen.

———————— Think about it: ————————

If the same power that raised Jesus from the dead lives in you, what are you waiting for, girl? Get over that fear and get busy telling others about Him!

THE OLD ME

At one time all of us lived to please our old selves. We gave in to what our bodies and minds wanted. We were sinful from birth like all other people and would suffer from the anger of God. But God had so much loving-kindness. He loved us with such a great love.

EPHESIANS 2:3–4

Some people have a before and after story, don't they, Jesus? They acted one way before they came to know You, then acted a different way after. That's because You change hearts and lives. You make people better than they used to be. When Your Holy Spirit comes to live inside us and we get to know You, we simply can't stay the same! We start changing to look more and more like You as we grow in our faith. I'm so glad the old me is in the past, Jesus! Amen.

──────── Think about it: ────────

What if you never changed? What if you never learned any lessons from life? What kind of adult would you be someday?

HOW I TREAT THEM MATTERS

"I say to you who hear Me, love those who work against you. Do good to those who hate you."
Luke 6:27

How I treat other people matters, Jesus—whether they're my friends or the people who bug me the most. When they say harsh words, my response matters. When they ignore me, my response matters. When they forget to invite me to their birthday party or other big event, my response matters. The reason my response matters is because the person matters. Even if they're not on their best behavior! After all, You keep right on loving me and treating me kindly even on the days when I ignore You. Make me more like You, I pray. Amen.

——————— Think about it: ———————

Why do you suppose it matters so much to God how you react to people when they've done something to hurt you?

YOU ARE NEAR, JESUS

Look for the Lord while He may be found.
Call upon Him while He is near.
ISAIAH 55:6

I don't have to look very far to find You, Jesus! Even when I'm sound asleep, You're right beside me, giving me sweet dreams and helping me get the rest I need to have a good day tomorrow. Sometimes I run off and You have to come looking for me, but I won't ever have to wonder where You are. When I call, You answer! You rush my way and say, "What's up, girl? Everything okay over here?" With You by my side, everything is truly okay. Amen.

——————— Think about it: ———————

When you get scared, who do you call for?
Your mom? Dad? Big brother? Jesus is even
closer, so call on Him when you're afraid.

THE BEST GUIDE

*For the Lord will be your trust. He will
keep your foot from being caught.*
PROVERBS 3:26

If I went on a long walk in a wilderness park, I would want a really good guide, someone who knew the way. A guide would know where the dangers were—deep holes in the path, bears in the woods, broken tree branches, and so on. With a guide leading the way, I would be super safe. That's what You are, Jesus. You're the best guide ever. You lay out my path, and I take safe steps, knowing You're right there, leading the way. You will keep my foot from going into a trap! Thanks for always guiding me. Amen.

——————— Think about it: ———————

If you headed out into the woods completely alone, would you feel safe? Why is having a guide so helpful?

Salvation is a Free Gift

For by His loving-favor you have been saved from the punishment of sin through faith. It is not by anything you have done. It is a gift of God.
EPHESIANS 2:8

Life is very expensive these days, Jesus! I hear my parents talking about how much it costs to buy groceries, gas, and clothes. They even worry about the electric bill! They're always telling me to turn off the lights. One thing that hasn't gone up in price is salvation. Giving my heart to You cost me nothing, but it cost You everything. You gave Your life on the cross so that I could be set free. It's because of Your loving-favor that You saved me. Thank You so much for Your great love. Amen.

─────── Think about it: ───────

What if Jesus charged a price for salvation?
Would we ever be able to pay it?

NO FEAR WHEN I SEE YOU

Our heart may say that we have done wrong.
But remember, God is greater than our heart.
He knows everything. Dear friends, if our
heart does not say that we are wrong, we will
have no fear as we stand before Him.
1 JOHN 3:20–21

I remember what it was like when I was little, Jesus. Every time I did something naughty, I hid from my parents. I knew they would be upset with me, so I didn't want to face them. Sometimes I'm still that way when I mess up. But I'm learning that You will still love me even when I've done something terrible. I don't have to be afraid to face You no matter how bad I've messed up. My heart will say, "You shouldn't have done that," but You, Lord? You're ready to forgive and forget. Thank You! Amen.

———————— Think about it: ————————

Why is God so quick to forgive?

EVERYTHING IN LOVE

Everything you do should be done in love.
1 CORINTHIANS 16:14

When You say "everything," Jesus, do You really mean *everything*? Like, when I talk to my mom, I should do that in love? And when I'm doing the dishes or clearing the table, I should do that in love too? When I'm working on my homework? When I'm helping Dad clean the garage? When I'm sitting next to that girl in science class who annoys me? Even then? I guess by "everything," You really do mean *everything*, so I'm going to try harder. Please help me to respond in love no matter what. Amen.

—————— Think about it: ——————

If you only treated people lovingly when you were in a good mood, what good would that be? Anyone can do that! You need to focus on loving others when you're having a hard day, girl!

YOU LOVE SO MUCH

"For God so loved the world that He gave His only Son. Whoever puts his trust in God's Son will not be lost but will have life that lasts forever."
JOHN 3:16

Wow, God! You must really, really love us. The Bible says You love us so much that You sent Your Son, Jesus, to die on the cross for us. He was Your only Son, and You gave Him for me. That gives me chills when I think about it! I don't ever want to forget the sacrifice You made for me. You love, so You gave. I want to be a giver too! Because I love others, I will learn to give. Amen.

――――――― Think about it: ―――――――

Why do you suppose God loves you so much? Is it because of something you've done, or is there another reason?

If I Claim to Love. . .

*Those who do not love do not know
God because God is love.*
1 John 4:8

If I claim to love other people, then I have to really love them, not just pretend. Oh, it's easy to say, "I love all people!" but do I really? Do I act like I love that kid in school who drives me crazy, teasing me? Do I act like I love my older sister when she won't let me borrow her stuff? Do I act like I love my parents when they make me clean my room? I can't go around claiming that I'm a loving person when I don't act like it. Help me when it's hard, pretty please? Thanks, Jesus! Amen.

—————— Think about it: ——————

No one ever said that loving people was
going to be easy. Who's the hardest
person for you to love sometimes?

I'M A GIVER

Each of you should give what you have decided in your heart to give, not reluctantly or under compulsion, for God loves a cheerful giver.
2 CORINTHIANS 9:7 NIV

You teach us that we should be givers, Jesus, and I am! It's so fun to give money in the offering plate at church, and it feels good to help take care of people who are going through a hard season. I won't give with a big frown on my face. No way! When I give, it will be with a huge smile and a song in my heart. That's how You must feel when You pour out blessings on Your kids. Are You singing over us as You shower down those blessings? Thanks for teaching me how to be a cheerful giver. Amen.

─────── Think about it: ───────

Which is more fun—to give cheerfully or to give with a frown? Always give with joy, girl!

YOU GIVE BACK

"Give, and it will be given to you. You will have more than enough. It can be pushed down and shaken together and it will still run over as it is given to you. The way you give to others is the way you will receive in return."

Luke 6:38

No matter how much I give, You always return it to me, Jesus! Like that time I gave away one of my favorite toys. Or that time my family gave to someone in need, and then, the next thing we knew, we were getting blessed in return. I like how You do math! You multiply things back to us. It's so fun. You promise that we'll never have to go without, and I know You're right. I've seen it time and time again. Thanks for pouring out blessings on us, Jesus. Amen.

Think about it:

You can't out-give God, but it might be fun to try! Who can you bless today?

It's Better to Give

"In every way I showed you that by working hard like this we can help those who are weak. We must remember what the Lord Jesus said, 'We are more happy when we give than when we receive.'"
Acts 20:35

I have to admit, I like to get stuff, Jesus. I really look forward to birthdays and Christmas when I get lots of cool things. It's not wrong to like gifts, but it's way more fun to give stuff away. I love to bless others, especially when they're feeling down or going through a rough time. Giving brings a smile to the face of the person who receives my gift. I love seeing that. Is that how You feel when You give good gifts to me? Do You see me smiling? I hope so! Amen.

—————— Think about it: ——————

Why do you suppose God says it makes us happier to give than receive?

I WON'T GIVE UP

*Do not let yourselves get tired of doing
good. If we do not give up, we will get what
is coming to us at the right time.*

GALATIANS 6:9

Sometimes I do the right thing, but it doesn't work out. I'm nice to someone who has been ugly to me. Or I decide not to cheat on a test even after the boy next to me in class tells me I should. But then things don't always end up right. The teacher thinks I'm cheating. The mean girl spreads ugly rumors about me. Still, I won't give up, Jesus. You say I should never get tired of doing the right thing—and I won't. Tonight, I'll go to sleep and wake up to a fresh, new day, ready to live for You. Amen.

——————— Think about it: ———————

Jesus always did the right thing, but He still faced troubles. What can you learn from His story?

FINAL WORDS

This is the last thing I want to say:
Be strong with the Lord's strength.
EPHESIANS 6:10

Sometimes I feel like a real weakling, Jesus. I'm not strong at all. The more people hurt me, the weaker I feel. Then I remember that my strength doesn't come from me. (Whew!) It's all from You, Lord! Even when I'm at my very weakest, You can make me strong enough to overcome any problem. Thank You for the strength You give. I can't wait to see what tomorrow looks like. You're going to use me to do great things. I'm sure of it! Amen.

───────── Think about it: ─────────

Even if you worked out at the gym and had giant muscles, you still wouldn't be any stronger spiritually, would you? Rest easy, girl! Your strength comes from God.

SCRIPTURE INDEX

OLD TESTAMENT

NEW TESTAMENT

CHECK OUT THESE OTHER GREAT BOOKS!

100 Extraordinary Stories for Courageous Girls

Girls are world changers! And this deeply inspiring storybook proves it! This collection of 100 extraordinary stories of women of faith—from the Bible, history, and today—will empower you to know and understand how women have made a difference in the world and how much smaller our faith (and the biblical record) would be without them.

Hardback / 978-1-68322-748-9

Cards of Kindness for Courageous Girls: Shareable Devotions and Inspiration

You will delight in spreading kindness and inspiration wherever you go with these shareable Cards of Kindness! Each perforated page features a just-right-sized devotional reading plus a positive life message that will both uplift and inspire your young heart.

Paperback / 978-1-64352-164-0

The Bible for Courageous Girls

Part of the exciting Courageous Girls series, this Bible provides complete Old and New Testament text in the easy-reading New Life Version, plus insert pages featuring full-color illustrations of bold, brave women such as Abigail, Deborah, Esther, Mary Magdalene, and Mary, mother of Jesus.

DiCarta / 978-1-64352-069-8